Front Porch Reflections

Devotions for Every Season

By Teresa Cleary

CPH.
SAINT LOUIS

Copyright © 2000 Teresa Cleary
Published by Concordia Publishing House
3558 S. Jefferson Avenue, St. Louis, MO 63118–3968
Manufactured in the United States of America

Library of Congress Cataloging-in-Publication Data

1 2 3 4 5 6 7 8 9 10   09 08 07 06 05 04 03 02 01 00

Dedication
To Tim, who has shared all my front porches, for believing.

Contents

Invitation 9

WINTER

THE SEASON OF GOD'S WARMTH

SPRING

THE SEASON OF NEW LIFE

SUMMER

THE SEASON OF LIGHT

AUTUMN
THE SEASON OF ABUNDANCE

CHRISTMAS
THE SEASON OF MY SAVIOR

Acknowledgments

God has blessed my life with many wonderful people. I would like to thank a few of them for their significant contributions to this book. Thank you ...

Tim, Micah, Steven, and Emily:
You are my greatest blessings! Thank you for giving me time to write and for letting me share your stories.

Bob Hostetler:
Your assistance in the initial stages of this project helped give it wings.

Jayne Reizner:
You shared the vision of this book from the very beginning and encouraged me every step of the way. You are a treasure!

Kathy Cassel, Judy Hershner, Catherine Hershberger, and Karen Hitchcock:
Your insights, enthusiasm, and gentle criticism improved this book immensely. Thank you for being so good to me!

Dawn Weinstock:
Your kindness and professionalism in walking a first-time book author through this process are greatly appreciated.

Members of the Greater Cincinnati Christian Writers' Fellowship:
You have supported me in all my projects. Thank you.

Above all else, thanks and praise are due to God Almighty, who meets me on my porch in every season and who gave life to this dream one page at a time. To Him be the glory!

My soul thirsts for God, for the living God.
When can I go and meet with God?
(Psalm 42:2)

INVITATION

In the corner of my front porch there hangs a swing. Its wooden slats are painted white, and its metal chains *clink* as they tighten under my weight. I settle on the seat and stretch my toe to give myself the push that will start the swing's rhythmic motion.

As I sway back and forth, I savor the crisp fall air that carries the musty smell of apples ready to be picked and the gentle song of wind chimes. In the distance, I hear the far-off cry of Canada geese as they make their way to our lake. I lean forward, anxious for a first glimpse of the birds. I watch as their dark forms come into view over the treetops. They dip their wings to circle the lake in their descent, glide across the water's surface, and skid to a halt. The geese exuberantly honk their greetings to all who care to listen. "We're home again!" they seem to announce. "It's great to be here!" I smile and lean back into the swing. I know exactly how they feel.

My front porch is my sanctuary. It's the place I go when I want to flee from the pressures of my life and just take some time—time to relax, to reflect, and to savor the moment at hand. As I sit there, I feel the tension in my shoulders lessen and the cares of my day recede. A soft breeze stirs. To me, it is the breath of God. It's His whisper of love telling me, "I am here." It is God's reassurance that He is always with me.

I think God gives all of us a desire for a quiet spot to call our own—a place to think, to dream, to celebrate, to rejoice, to weep, to deepen our knowledge and sense of who we are and whose we are. We all need a place in addition to His sanctuary where we can go to meet with God, to hear Him speak into our hearts through His Word, and to reflect on how He is acting in our lives.

If you have a front porch of your own, whether it's a concrete stoop or a wide veranda, I encourage you to use it as often as possible. Make it a special place where you can spend time daily with your heavenly Father. If you don't have a front porch, I encourage you to make one for yourself. It can be the steps of your trailer, a spot next to a window in your apartment, or your favorite chair. This is your place to relax, sit quietly, and spend time with the Lord. I've found that as I sit on my front porch, my agenda fades away, and God's agenda takes over. I crumple my "to do" list and wait on the Lord.

But waiting is really too passive a word for what happens. My front porch is a place where I acknowledge God's importance in my life and actively seek His guidance. As I meditate on God's Word, my heavenly Father instructs, admonishes, praises, reproofs, and encourages me. Sometimes His words are gentle; sometimes they are not. Yet I always come away from this time with the assurance that God loves me, forgives me for Jesus' sake, and has a plan for this day, even for my life.

The seat next to me on the swing is always open. Won't you join me? We'll watch the days come and go and rejoice in what the Lord has in store for us in each new season of our lives. As we sit, we'll hear God's voice through His Book and enjoy the comfort of His presence. For here, like everywhere, God is with us. We are never truly alone.

WINTER

The Season of God's Warmth

He sends the snow in all its lovely whiteness,
and scatters the frost upon the ground.
(Psalm 147:16 TLB)

"For I know the plans I have for you," declares the LORD.
(Jeremiah 29:11)

CELEBRATION

I open the door that leads to my front porch and step out into a world transformed. Snow falls from the sky like white confetti, settling softly on the grass and the branches of the pear trees. As I walk over to the porch swing, I see that it, too, is covered with a cold thin blanket.

I pull my coat collar up around my ears and shiver as I take in the morning quiet of the winter-white world around me. Dusting the snow off the swing, I feel the cold penetrate the fabric of my gloves. I sit down and marvel at this perfect picture of the fresh beginning I've prayed for to start my new year. "Thank You, Lord," I whisper, "for this day, this time, this place."

I push my toe against the porch floor to start the swing's rhythmic rocking and continue to look around. It hasn't been cold enough for the lake in our front yard to freeze, and our five white ducks are swimming around in close formation. I smile as the air is suddenly filled with their exuberant quacking. They seem to be voicing their approval of the celebration being thrown around them.

As I sit on my swing, I am celebrating too. This party, though, is nothing like the raucous event of the night before. This morning there are no pots and pans being banged by my three children, no fireworks lit by their exuberant dad, and no friendly shouts of "Happy New Year!" as we all celebrate when the clock strikes midnight. I smile as I remember the warmth of the hugs we all exchanged as the old year was ushered out and the new year was ushered in. I know deep in my heart that each year that God gives us is cause for thanksgiving and rejoicing.

This morning's celebration, though, is even more to my liking. It is quieter, more peaceful. This is my own private party. The only guest I've invited is the Lord. Here on the porch, with no one else around, we'll celebrate the coming of a new year.

With the Holy Spirit's help, I'll dedicate the days ahead to accomplishing my heavenly Father's work and His will. I'll give thanks for new beginnings, draw comfort in God's closeness to me, discover insights from His Word, delight in life's simple pleasures, and share dreams of what lies ahead. God's words tell me that I am a new creation in Christ (2 Corinthians 5:17). Through Baptism's cleansing waters, I share in Jesus' victory over sin and death. The beginning of a new year is the perfect time to refocus on a life that reflects that high calling.

As this new year begins, I cling to God's promise from Jeremiah: "And I know the plans I have for you," declares the LORD, "plans to prosper you and not to harm you, plans to give you hope and a future." I am assured that no matter what lies ahead, God and I will go through it together. My days—my year—are in God's hand. I trust in His promise that "you will seek Me and find Me when you seek Me with all your heart" (Jeremiah 29:13).

Today is a new day, the start of a new year, and I know God has cleansed my heart and made it His. That, above all, is cause for celebration.

Prayer: Father of new beginnings, I dedicate not only this day, but this entire year, to You. May each step of the journey ahead give me cause for celebration. Remind me often that You always walk beside me. In Jesus' name. Amen.

Reflection: As this new year begins, pray for God to reveal the plans He has for you in the year ahead.

I will instruct you and teach you in the way you should go; I will counsel you and watch over you. (Psalm 32:8)

MY GUIDE

Bright sunshine greets me this morning as I open the front door and take a deep breath of the cold, clean air. *Good morning, Lord!* my heart says. *Thank You for this beautiful day!*

I head over to the porch swing and put my Bible down on the seat beside me. The quietness that greets me is a welcome gift. School has been back in session for a few days now after two hectic weeks of Christmas vacation. We are all readjusting to getting up early, and Micah and Steven, both in grade school, are once again spending part of their evenings doing homework. Emily, only in preschool, likes to sit with her brothers and work on her own projects as the boys study.

Over the past few nights, I've answered quite a few calls from the boys for help with a math problem here or a spelling word there. While answering homework questions for Steven is easy, I'm thankful Micah has remembered to bring his math book home with him. There have been a few times I've had to give his textbook a quick glance to refresh my memory before answering his question.

This morning, though, there are no questions. I have a

few quiet minutes to myself. I pick up my Bible and let it fall open to where the marker keeps my place.

As this new year begins, I'm thankful to have my own textbook readily available. Not only is the Bible where I turn for comfort and encouragement and for answers to life's questions, for me it's life itself (John 6:68). In its pages, I've learned about God and found the answer to my most pressing need. As I've read these words and listened to them in God's house, the Holy Spirit has given me faith in Jesus, my Savior, and taught me of God's merciful love.

With the many days that stretch ahead of me this year, I'm grateful that God promises to instruct me and teach me in the way I should go (Psalm 32:8), and I am confident He will accomplish this through His Word. I know that "all Scripture is God-breathed and is useful for teaching, rebuking, correcting and training in righteousness, so that the man of God may be thoroughly equipped for every good work" (2 Timothy 3:16).

As I begin reading my Bible, I ask God to open my mind and my heart to what He has for me within the pages of His Word. I pray I will be a lifetime learner and that the Lord always will be my teacher.

Prayer: Father, I thank You for Your life-giving Word. Through it, the Holy Spirit works in my life—revealing my need for a Savior, pointing me to Jesus, calling me to repentance, assuring me of forgiveness, and strengthening my faith. In my Savior's name. Amen.

Reflection: What message does God have in His Word for you today?

He sends the snow in all its lovely whiteness, and scatters the frost upon the ground. (Psalm 147:16 TLB)

WHITER THAN SNOW

A pristine coat of white covers our yard this morning. No one has ventured outside, so no footprints mar the surface, no sled tracks carve parallel marks on the crust.

As I look around the yard, I am amazed at how well the snow has hidden the imperfections that I know lie beneath its covering. There's the area by the maple trees that stays wet most of the year. In the spring and fall, it's a muddy mess. In the summer, it's a brown eyesore in the middle of the yard. Then there are the bare spots in the front lawn. My husband, Tim, waged a good fight all last summer, but he couldn't seem to get grass to grow in those places. Last, but not least, is the area by the fence where the ducks and geese congregate as they wait for a neighbor to arrive with a daily bucket of feed. The birds have trampled every last bit of grass there.

Today all those imperfections are hidden. Our yard looks perfect—at least for the moment.

Then I realize I'm hiding those same kinds of imperfections under the surface of my life. While it may appear on the outside that everything is running smoothly, on the inside are my own "muddy spots" of sin. Whether it's my tendency to gossip, my judgmental attitude, or my quick temper, I'm very likely trying to white out my own dark sins.

That's why I'm so thankful for the sight before me. It's a physical reminder of the Lord's promise to me: "Though your sins are like scarlet, they shall be as white as snow; though they are red as crimson, they shall be like wool" (Isaiah 1:18).

Jesus came to purchase and win me from all sins, from death, and from the power of the devil. He came that I might be brought into the family of my heavenly Father despite the fact that God is perfect and I am so totally imperfect. He came so the crimson of my sin would be washed away and made white by His blood shed on the cross for me. He came so I could live forever with Him because of His resurrection.

I know that soon my children will clamor for me to join them outside to ride their sleds or build a snowman. As we tramp through the yard, the perfect surface will be broken, and the whiteness will turn to gray. Even so, I will rejoice that Jesus has made me whiter than snow, and I am His forever.

Prayer: Heavenly Father, I stand before You in the blackness of my sin and ask Your forgiveness for all I've done to displease You. Give me Your strength to walk in Your way. Guide my choices to reflect Jesus, my Savior. In His name I pray. Amen.

Reflection: What will you confess to the Lord so He can make your sins whiter than snow?

By wisdom a house is built, and through understanding it is established;
through knowledge its rooms are filled with rare and beautiful treasures.
(Proverbs 24:3–4)

HOME IS WHERE THE HEART IS

Day after day as I sit out here on the porch, I silently thank God for this wonderful place called home. For my family it is a safe haven, a resting place, a welcome refuge. We call it our *Bethany* because it is the place where we step back from the world, just as Jesus retreated to the home of Mary and Martha in Bethany when He needed time away from the crowds.

Our home is the place our family shares meals and confidences. It is where we work and play, argue and forgive, praise and encourage. For us, our home is so much more than the walls that surround us because it is made up of the love we have for one another. Most important, our home is built on the solid foundation of Jesus Christ. He is our cornerstone, and we truly believe that "unless the LORD builds the house, its builders labor in vain" (Psalm 127:1).

From the day we moved in, our home has been dedicated to the Lord and has been used in His service. We have hosted family, friends, and even strangers as we "serve one another in love" (Galatians 5:13). We pray that those who cross its threshold will find even a small measure of comfort and caring in this place so they may walk away refreshed.

As wonderful as our home is, we are learning not to hold too tightly to this earthly abode because, as Christians, we realize this present world isn't really our home. We know God has for us "an eternal house in heaven, not built by human hands" (2 Corinthians 5:1). It is a place where, we are promised, God "will wipe every tear from [our] eyes. There will be no more death or mourning or crying or pain, for the old order of things has passed away" (Revelation 21:4).

This contrasting lesson of our earthly home and our heavenly home has been a wonderful way to teach my children that the things of importance in life are those things that matter for eternity. Like my children, there are times I need to ask God to relax my grip on my earthly treasures and begin the work of storing up treasures in heaven "where moth and rust do not destroy, and where thieves do not break in and steal" (Matthew 6:20). Ultimately, heaven is our home, and that is where I want our hearts to be.

Prayer: Jesus, I thank You that You have prepared a place for me where I will spend eternity with You. Amen.

Reflection: Are you living a life that is focused on those things that are of eternal importance?

He says to the snow, "Fall on the earth." (Job 37:6)

S N O W D A Y

The word came early this morning that the schools are closed. The huge, cotton ball snowflakes that fell last night have left six inches of ice-cold fluff everywhere. The streets are too slippery for school buses to travel through, and it will be hours before the snowplow makes it to our neighborhood. My children are ecstatic.

Emily stands at the kitchen window drawing pictures in the mist her breath leaves on the glass. Outside, the snow lies like a smooth white page ready to be written on. "Everyone into your snowsuits!" I call, thinking of the story we'll create during the time we'll spend outside. "We're going to make a snowman." My announcement is greeted with whoops of joy and the sound of running feet.

As we step outside, the brightness of the day is almost blinding. We all give our eyes a minute to adjust to the light before bounding down the steps and into the yard. Emily begins twirling around the yard like a snowflake while the boys start packing snowballs and lobbing them at each other. I look around. The trees by the lake look as though they have been painted white. The bench underneath them, which usually holds people, has only snow in its lap today. Beyond the lake, the houses in the neighborhood look as though they're huddling together for warmth.

All around, the smooth, white snow invites us to write our names on its surface. "Watch this!" I say, dragging my feet to form the letters of my name. Soon "T-e-r-e-s-a" is written in large letters across the front yard. The boys quickly start their own names while Emily trails after me to spell hers. When we're finished, we all run to the top of the porch steps to admire our handiwork. Our yard definitely has a personalized look to it.

"Time for the snowman!" I call.

"How about a snow family?" Steven asks. "One for each of us."

We all agree that it's a great idea, and the work begins. Snowballs roll across the yard, growing bigger with each turn. Sometimes it takes Micah and me working together to lift the cold globes high enough to place them on top of one another, but we get the job done. In an hour our work is finished. Our snow family stands together, looking out across the lake. They seem to be welcoming visitors, inviting them to come and play.

"Can we go in and have hot chocolate now?" Steven asks. "I'm cold."

"Me too," Emily and Micah agree.

While the children head inside to get warm, I linger on the porch. I recall a favorite Bible passage: "This is the day the LORD has made, let us rejoice and be glad in it" (Psalm 118:24).

"Thank You, Lord," I whisper, "for ordinary days that become special when shared with those I love." I look out past our snow family to the few places in the yard where we haven't walked or played this morning. Suddenly the sun touches those surfaces, making them sparkle like diamonds. I nod my head and smile. I knew all along there was treasure to be found out here.

Prayer: Heavenly Father, in Your grace You already have given me so much more than I deserve. In addition to all Your other good gifts, I thank You for days that sparkle like diamonds. Amen.

Reflection: What reason to rejoice has God given you this day?

I will say of the LORD, "He is my refuge and my fortress, my God, in whom I trust." (Psalm 91:2)

THE BATTLE

Late yesterday afternoon when Tim got home from work, he and the boys, along with some friends, dragged five-gallon buckets into the front yard. They filled these with snow, packed it in tightly, carefully turned the buckets over to remove the frozen bricks, then piled the ice-cold circles on top of one another.

The walls went up quickly, and before long two snow forts took shape on either side of the front sidewalk. After the work was complete, there wasn't much time for battle, so a temporary truce was called because of the early darkness.

Today, though, is Saturday, and there's a battle being waged in our front yard. My boys were outside bright and early. It wasn't long before their friends, Aaron and Josiah, joined them, and the battle raged. Snowballs have been flying back and forth between the forts most of the morning. Sometimes these brave warriors hit their targets. Sometimes they don't. Their energy is inexhaustible, and with six inches of snow on the ground, so is their ammunition.

As I watch the boys from the safe shelter of the porch,

I'm reminded of the daily battles waged deep inside my heart. Some of them involve small temptations—like whether I'll eat those chocolate chip cookies that seem to be calling my name from the pantry. Others involve more serious ones—like whether I'll unleash my quick temper on my children or whether I will indulge in a round of gossip with a friend. Yet no matter if the temptations I face are big or small, there's always some battle to fight. I either give in to the enticement of sin or, by God's grace, I stand firm. Sometimes, God helps me to walk away. Other times, I stumble and fall.

What I'm learning is when temptation starts, I can ask for the Lord's help in dealing with it (1 Corinthians 10:13). Facing my problems isn't something I can do alone. God gives me His strength to face those areas of my life that lead me into sin. He gives me the protection of the One who is the "rock of refuge to which I can always go" (Psalm 71:3).

The battle in the front yard seems to have ceased for the moment. I wish the same could be said for my battles. Yet I know God is my fortress, and His Holy Spirit will help me fight off the attacks of temptation. Behind His protective walls of love, I'll be safe.

Prayer: Lord, You are my rock and my fortress. Forgive me for the times I yield to temptation. Lead me through all the temptations I face, for when I am weak, You are strong. In Your name. Amen.

Reflection: Have you asked for the Lord's help in overcoming the temptations you face right now?

Pray for each other.
(James 5:16)

PRAYER LIST

I pull a folded piece of notebook paper from the front of my Bible and glance over the names and requests I've written down. My latest prayer list isn't very long, but I know it will be only a matter of time before that changes. As I keep my ears open and my heart soft, I find there are new requests to add to my list almost daily.

The squeak of the porch swing sets my pace as I read each name and each situation. With some, the face of a friend or family member comes to mind. With others, I am praying for a stranger whose life has been turned upside down. These people don't know me and I don't know them, but someone who cares for them asked me to pray—and so I do. It is a privilege I take seriously.

I've had quite a few prayer lists over the years. My lists have ranged from small requests for safety or comfort to catalogs of sickness, marital problems, deep need, and crisis. Yet for all the pain and sorrow written there, these prayer records are also full of God's healing, God's intervention, and God's miracles. Time and again, my prayer lists have shown me how God is intimately involved in the lives of His people. Time and again, I see that the Lord who cares for the birds of the air cares even more deeply for His children (Matthew 6:26).

Yet I've also learned that putting a situation in the Lord's hands doesn't necessarily mean He'll answer my prayer in the way I think He should. Many times over the years God has said no when I was sure He would say yes. Other times I've felt God's call to wait when I wanted—and wanted Him—to charge ahead. I've learned firsthand the truth of the Bible passage: " 'For My thoughts are not your thoughts, neither are your ways My ways,' declares the LORD" (Isaiah 55:8). When it comes to prayer, I can't put God on a timetable or second-guess His response. What my prayer lists have clearly shown me over and over again is that I can't lean on my own understanding. Instead I can trust God with my whole heart (Proverbs 3:5). I can echo Jesus' prayer in the garden that God's will would be done.

As God has strengthened my trust in Him, I've seen Him give "a crown of beauty instead of ashes, the oil of gladness instead of mourning, and a garment of praise instead of a spirit of despair" (Isaiah 61:3). In my lifetime I've rejoiced over miraculous healings and praised the Lord over dying marriages made alive again.

I'll admit that God's answers aren't always easy to understand, and the way He leads isn't always easy to follow. But I know I'd rather walk through life's troubles beside my Lord than to walk through life's joys without Him. So today on the porch I say a prayer for each person on my list. I pray that they will know and trust in God's presence in their lives and that they, too, will know they don't walk alone.

Prayer: Heavenly Father, I thank You for the privilege of coming before Your throne with my needs and requests and with the needs and requests of others. I thank You even more that You answer each prayer in the way that is best. In Jesus' name. Amen.

Reflection: A prayer list can be a visible record of God's work in your life and in the lives of others. If you don't keep one, why not start today?

Faith is the substance of things hoped for,
the evidence of things not seen.
(Hebrews 11:1 KJV)

THE FIRE OF FAITH

This afternoon the ducks are huddled together against the cold wind that blows across the yard. They look like piles of snow in the grass, and I wonder if they are a sign of things to come. *No more snow please,* I think, as I remember the hours I've already spent shoveling mounds of the white stuff from the driveway and sidewalks.

I wish I had someone to huddle with on my swing, but Tim is at work and the children aren't home from school yet. I have only my coat to keep me warm, and even its thick layers are no match for the winter weather. "Lord, this isn't my favorite season," I confess through teeth that want to chatter. The whistling wind snatches my words and carries them into the yard. It shakes the branches of the trees until they seem to dance.

If only the season were as short as the daylight hours are, I lament, thinking of all the evenings of early darkness that are still to come. There already have been too many times this season when I've been driven into the house by bitter cold temperatures and frosty northern winds. Today, though, I refuse to give up my time on the porch. Instead,

I light a fire of determination within myself and resolve to outlast the frigid weather.

Part of my determination comes from another fire that burns deep within me. It's the fire of faith, the flame God's Spirit started at my Baptism and keeps glowing steadily inside my heart. It's faith that tells me even on the darkest winter night that God is with me, that Jesus is "the light [that] shines in the darkness" (John 1:5). It's faith that trusts in forgiveness for all my sins because of my Savior's sacrifice. It's faith that celebrates a promised heavenly reward. It's faith that helps me know that even on the coldest winter day, the warmth of God's love is available to all those who call on His name.

While I know the Lord is faithful in every season, it is during the winter that the promise of His presence gives me the most hope for the days to come. I echo the Scriptures as I declare to the Lord, "Thou art my hope" (Jeremiah 17:17 KJV). Through the dark and through the cold, the Holy Spirit keeps the flame of my faith burning brightly.

Prayer: Heavenly Father, I've found that the cold winter winds that blow through my life have only served to drive me closer to You and the warmth of Your embrace. Thank You for the love You show me in Christ during every season of the year. In His name I pray. Amen.

Reflection: How does the Lord stir the fire of faith that burns inside of you?

Therefore God exalted Him to the highest place and gave Him the name that is above every name, that at the name of Jesus every knee should bow, in heaven and on earth and under the earth. (Philippians 2:9–10)

BOWING DOWN

A winter storm came through our city last night and coated everything outside in a slippery layer of ice. From inside the house, I can the see the sun's rays shining brightly on the clear, hard surfaces. The beauty of it all draws me from the warmth of the kitchen to the cold outside. As I carefully make my way across the porch, I hear the ice crunching under my feet.

The rocking chairs and swing are too slippery to use, so I stand at the porch rail and take in this ice-covered world. Icicles of all lengths hang in rows from the gutters. The crystal clear coldness covers the pear trees in the front yard, as well as the birch and maples on the side of the house. It also encases our bushes and plants, the iron bench, and the picket fence, turning them all into works of art. Everywhere I turn there is ice.

Looking around, I notice a decided droop to all the trees in the yard. Out by the lake, four weeping willows are bent almost to the ground under the weight of the ice that covers them. From my vantage point, it looks as if all of nature is bowing down before the awesome majesty of the

Lord. As I stand there, I bow my head and join in that worship as God's Word floods my mind.

This is the day the LORD has made; let us rejoice and be glad in it. (Psalm 118:24)

Holy, holy, holy is the LORD Almighty: the whole earth is full of His glory. (Isaiah 6:3)

From the rising of the sun to the place where it sets, the name of the LORD is to be praised. (Psalm 113:3)

Ascribe to the LORD the glory due His name. (1 Chronicles 16:29)

Yours, O LORD, is the greatness and the power and the glory and the majesty and the splendor, for everything in heaven and earth is Yours. (1 Chronicles 29:11)

You are worthy, our Lord and God, to receive glory and honor and power, for You created all things, and by Your will they were created and have their being. (Revelation 4:11)

I stand with my head bowed for a few minutes more, letting the quiet of the morning settle deep within me. When I open my eyes again, I am struck anew at the beauty around me. "Our God reigns!" my heart sings along with the wind that whistles through the trees. "Our God reigns!"

Prayer: Heavenly Father, even though my words are inadequate to give You the honor You deserve, please accept the humble offering of my praise. In Jesus' name. Amen.

Reflection: How will you praise the Lord today?

And my God will meet all your needs according to His glorious riches in Christ Jesus. (Philippians 4:19)

GOD'S PROVISION

Feeding the ducks is a ritual at my house. At some point during the day, I gather together the last pieces of bread from the bottom of the bread bag, some unfinished popcorn from the night before, or stale dinner rolls that have languished in the back of the refrigerator. With my provisions in place, I pull on my coat and head out to the porch.

Whether it's the sound of my steps on the wooden boards or the sight of me with my handful of goodies, the ducks seem to anticipate my arrival and already are heading across the yard toward me as I take a seat on the top step. I can't help but smile as their waddling becomes a comic, joyful dance. Their bodies rock from side to side as they race across the yard at a speed that makes them look as if they are going to tip head over heels and somersault the rest of the way toward me.

While their quacks of greeting are enthusiastic all through the spring, summer, and autumn, now that it's winter, the noise borders on exuberance. Food is scarce and not as many of our neighbors venture out of their warm homes to feed the ducks as did in the summer when the weather beckons everyone outside. So the ducks have come to rely on me—to trust my provision for them. They believe I'll be there, and I do my best not to disappoint them.

Taking care of these creatures helps me better understand part of God's care for me. Just as the ducks trust in my presence and provision for them each day, I trust that my heavenly Father, will be there to meet all my needs, even as He already has met my greatest need by sending Jesus to be my Savior from sin.

There are times, though, when my actions are the opposite of the truth that rests in my heart. Too often I race toward God with my neck outstretched, "quacking" my requests as loudly as possible to be sure I'm heard over the "quacking" of the person next to me. Do I think God doesn't hear me? Do I believe He'll ignore me in favor of someone else? Do I imagine He doesn't already know what I need?

No matter what I may think or feel at the moment, I know what the Bible tells me is true. God is there, ready to hear my prayers and provide His best for me. His promise throughout Scripture is that He will be there every moment, every day, all the time (Hebrews 13:5). Unlike me, the Lord never forgets or gets too busy or runs out of what I need.

As I feed the ducks this winter, God is teaching me some important lessons. I see how God is at work through His Word and through His Sacrament to strengthen my trust in His provision for my physical and spiritual life. I see how God is encouraging me to lean more on Him and less on myself. I see how faith is, indeed, "being sure of what we hope for and certain of what we do not see" (Hebrews 11:1). I see that, by the power of His Holy Spirit, I can say, "No matter what, Lord, I trust you." I see that God is dependable. He is trustworthy. He is reliable. In a world of uncertainty, God is a sure thing. That gives me hope—a hope I can walk in with confidence.

Prayer: Thank You, heavenly Father, for Your availability every minute, every hour, every day. Thank You for the gift of faith. I put my hope, my trust, and my life in Your hands, knowing You are committed to my good. In Jesus' name. Amen.

Reflection: What has God provided for you recently that you can thank Him for?

Trust in the LORD forever, for the LORD, the LORD,
is the Rock eternal. (Isaiah 26:4)

TRUST

The endless gray days of winter have arrived, and the sky is leaden with clouds. There have been too many dismal days in a row, and my body and spirit cry out for the warmth and brightness of sunlight. Sitting here this afternoon, I hope against hope for even a peek of sunshine. All I want is one tiny ray to break through the clouds above. All I want is to see and feel the sun again. "Just for a moment, Lord?" I ask. The sun, though, refuses to budge from its hiding place.

Although the sun remains hidden, I know one day it will shine on me again. I have faith that the sun I can't see still shines. Moments like this remind me of how the Holy Spirit helps me trust God. How God's gift of faith in Christ assures me that my heavenly Father is working—surely and steadily, in His own way and in His own time—to accomplish His purposes in my life. How I walk "by faith, not by sight" (2 Corinthians 5:7).

It's during the days when doubts nibble at my heart and mind that I turn to my Bible to hear again God's words of promise. In the pages of His book, I read of a God who is "changeless in His love for me" (Psalm 59:10 TLB). His

Word assures me that "in all things God works for the good of those who love Him, who have been called according to His purpose" (Romans 8:28). It touches my heart to know "blessed is he who trusts in the LORD" (Proverbs 16:20).

I sit outside on this gray winter day, knowing the sun may remain behind the clouds for quite a few days more. Somehow, that's all right. In the absence of the sun, God's Word brightens my darkness and drives those gray clouds of doubt away.

Prayer: Heavenly Father, when my faith is weak, help me to cling to Your promise that You "will keep in perfect peace him whose mind is steadfast, because he trusts in You" (Isaiah 26:3). In my Savior's name I pray. Amen.

Reflection: In what areas of your life do you need to ask God for an extra measure of trust in His unseen actions on your behalf?

God is love. (1 John 4:16)

VALENTINES

It's Valentine's Day, and even though the temperature outside is cold, I feel warm all over. It's a warmth that comes from knowing that God has blessed me beyond measure through the love of my family.

I reach into my pocket and pull out the cards I received this morning from Tim and the children. There is Emily's "handful of love" made from her own handprint; Steven's red construction paper heart that he made at school; Micah's small, store-bought card with his favorite superhero on the front; and Tim's pretty, foil-embossed reminder that he'd marry me all over again. While my husband is free with his "I love yous," my children's cards are a treasure because they represent sentiments that are too often left unspoken. I cherish these paper reminders of the bond of love we share.

As I put the cards back in my pocket, I pick up another Valentine. This one was written thousands of years ago, yet it is still the most beautiful love letter any person could ever receive. Line after line speaks of a Father's commitment to and love for His children. Within its pages, I have found a love that "covers over all wrongs" (Proverbs 10:12), "drives out fear" (1 John 4:18), and even caused one sinless

Man to "lay down His life for His friends" (John 15:13). Reading about such love is inspiring. Experiencing such love is overwhelming.

Within this letter, I also have found a model of love for my own life: "Love is patient, love is kind. It does not envy, it does not boast, it is not proud. It is not rude, it is not self-seeking, it is not easily angered, it keeps no record of wrongs. Love does not delight in evil but rejoices with the truth. It always protects, always trusts, always hopes, always perseveres" (1 Corinthians 13:4–7). These words set a high standard—one I could never reach on my own, but one that God helps me strive toward through the work of His Spirit in my life.

Even more than just setting the standard for love, God provided the world with its greatest example when He gave His Son, Jesus, to bridge the gap that our sin had created between us and Him. Because of a Father's great love, His children were returned to a blessed relationship with Him.

Day by day I'm learning from God's unconditional love that was shown for me on a wooden cross and that proclaimed victory over sin and the grave. I'm learning to love others, to love myself, and, above all, to love the Lord with all my heart and with all my soul and with all my strength (Deuteronomy 6:5).

Prayer: Heavenly Father, may today be about more than hearts and flowers. May it be a reminder to each of us of the tremendous love You show to us through Jesus. Amen.

Reflection: What valentine is God sending you today?

The LORD is my strength and my shield; my heart trusts in Him,
and I am helped. (Psalm 28:7)

A Taste of Spring

Today I enjoy an annual event—unseasonably warm weather for this time of year. Every February, about midway through the month, the temperature soars from somewhere in the 20s to 60 degrees or higher. In addition, the sky turns a brilliant blue, and fluffy, white clouds chase one another across its expanse. Although there are still small, dirty patches of snow on the ground, I know they won't be there for long. The breeze that caresses my cheek whispers "spring." In the middle of winter, days like this are a gift from God.

This taste of the upcoming season draws me out of the cocoon I've wrapped around myself during the winter. I stretch out my hands to feel the warmth and breathe deeply the sweet, damp air. As I sit here, I feel the sun's rays penetrate my clothes to warm my skin. Those rays seem to be reaching deeper—trying to touch my heart, my soul even.

The isolation of winter has brought out the worst in my do-it-myself attitude. Until now, I didn't realize that in many ways that attitude extended even to my spiritual life. Too often in the loneliness of winter, I haven't given my problems and concerns over to the Lord. Instead I've hugged them to myself like an old coat, not acknowledging that the warmth of God's love and the sincerity of His grace are a much better covering. I've forgotten that Jesus invites me to bring all my burdens to Him so He can give me His easy yoke instead (Matthew 11:28–30).

Today I accept that invitation. As I feel the chill of winter recede, I also feel the heaviness of my burdens lift as Jesus shoulders their weight for me. I know that winter is not yet over. I know, too, that more snow will fall before this season ends. Even so, I bask in the unexpected warmth of this day and in this small taste of heaven that God has sent my way.

Prayer: Heavenly Father, thank You for caring enough to send warm and sunny days like this. They are an unexpected blessing and are just enough to see me through the cold darkness of winter. Thank You, too, for sending Jesus to carry my burden of sin to the cross and leave it there. The faith in Him that you have given to me is a light and joyous yoke. In Jesus' name. Amen.

Reflection: Are there burdens you are trying to carry that you can give to Jesus?

My times are in Your hands. (Psalm 31:15)

EARLY BLOSSOMS

From the steps where I sit, I can see the first green tips of hyacinths starting to break through the hard, brown earth. Amidst the cold and snow of winter, there have been a few unseasonably warm days lately. Although the breeze holds the promise of spring, I know the start of the next season is still far off. Even so, the higher temperatures apparently have been enough to start the hyacinth bulbs growing before their time. I'm sure before long the daffodils and tulips will make an early appearance too.

"Stop!" I want to warn. "It's too early!" I even consider throwing dirt on top of the green shoots to protect them from the colder weather already forecast for the days ahead. In the end, though, I decide not to interfere.

There are other instances when I know I should choose to do nothing. These are instances when instead of minding my own business, I try to force God's plans to bloom too early, when I want to walk through doors He hasn't opened to me, and when I try to second-guess the direction He wants me to travel. There are other times when I attempt to cut back the blossoms that are flowering in my life, when I seek to shut the doors the Lord has opened, and when I try to apply the brakes at the same time God is stepping on the gas to move me forward.

Why is it that even though I know God holds the entire universe in His hands, keeps His many promises, and provides all I need, including faith and salvation, I still have a tendency to try to take charge? Is it a lack of trust? A fear of where the Lord might lead by His Spirit? A need to keep control firmly in my own hands? At one time or another in my life, the answer to all those questions has been yes.

Yet the more God increases my trust in Him, the more I see His guiding presence in my life. It quickly becomes apparent that God's plans for me are better than any plans I could dream up for myself. When it comes to God's work in my life, I can rejoice that "as for God, His way is perfect" (2 Samuel 22:31). The Lord doesn't need my help—or my interference—because "I know that everything God does will endure forever; nothing can be added to it and nothing taken from it" (Ecclesiastes 3:14).

God knows everything—from the smallest detail in my life to how many hyacinths have begun to sprout. Even as He tends to the fields and the birds, He will watch over me because He has made me His precious child through the waters of Baptism.

Prayer: Heavenly Father, because of the faith in Christ that You have given to me, I can proclaim that You are Lord of the universe and Lord of my life. Lead me daily by Your Spirit in the way You have laid out for me. In Jesus' name. Amen.

Reflection: How will you ask God to help you avoid leaping ahead of or holding back from His plans for you?

This is how we know what love is: Jesus Christ laid down His life for us.
(1 John 3:16)

CLEARING A PATH

After hours of high winds and snowflakes flying as fast as duck feathers, the latest winter storm finally has subsided. The snow outside again lies six inches thick on the ground. Tim and the boys bundle up in their coats, hats, and gloves and head outside to clear the driveway and the sidewalks. If we owned more shovels, Emily and I would be out there too.

After about an hour, I put on my coat and go outside to check their progress. Standing on the porch, I notice that the boys have the steps and sidewalk clear. Tim has used the tractor to make his way up our long driveway, and I can see it's almost entirely done. "How about some hot chocolate?" I call, hoping to be heard over the roar of the tractor.

Tim cuts the motor and puts his hand to his ear. I repeat my question.

"Just give us a few more minutes," he replies. "Then we'll be in."

Before I go back into the house, I admire all the hard work that has been done in the last hour. It's comforting to know the boys won't slip and slide their way down the driveway on the way to school, and we all have a safe way out to the street. Because of their hard work, everyone will benefit.

The path I see cleared in the snow reminds me of another path that was cleared for me—the path to the heavenly Father cleared by His Son, Jesus. Over and over in Holy Scripture, I am reminded of my sin, of my need for a Savior, and of Christ's sacrifice on my behalf. Romans 5:8 tells me clearly: "But God demonstrates His own love for us in this: While we were still sinners, Christ died for us." My sin separated me from my heavenly Father. There was no chance of making my way to Him on my own. Yet through the sacrifice of His Son, God the Father provided the solution. Jesus cleared the path between God and His children—me included. I'm humbled to think that "the Son of Man did not come to be served, but to serve, and to give His life as a ransom for many" (Matthew 20:28).

What should be my response to God's great gift? The answer to that comes from God's Word itself: "Live a life of love, just as Christ loved us and gave Himself up for us as a fragrant offering and sacrifice to God" (Ephesians 5:2). With God's help and through the work of His Spirit in my life, I can love those around me even as God in Christ has loved me.

Prayer: Heavenly Father, I thank You for sending Your Son, Jesus, to clear the obstacles that keep me from You. In His name I pray. Amen.

Reflection: What blocks your path to God right now?

"Let the little children come to Me, ...
for the kingdom of God belongs to such as these." (Mark 10:14)

A Child's Joy

After five minutes of bundling Emily up in an extra pair of socks, blue jeans over her knit pants, a snowsuit, boots, and her coat, hat, mittens, and scarf, I grab my coat and quietly follow my daughter outside. While I stop on the porch, Emily lumbers down the steps and out into the yard.

My daughter is oblivious to my gaze as I enjoy her antics. I almost laugh out loud as she races out into the snow and purposely falls face forward into a drift as if it were a fluffy, white pillow. The sound that comes from her mouth isn't the shriek of pain I expect, but one of delight. Her giggles continue as she rolls over and over across the yard as if trying to smooth out the lumps and wrinkles in the snow.

After a minute or two of these hijinks, Emily picks herself up and tramps through the yard in search of a new adventure. Not surprisingly, one never seems far off.

Next, I watch as Emily walks over to her pink plastic sled and lies down on top of it. After a bit of vigorous wiggling, she whoops with joy as the sled slowly slides down the slight incline in our side yard. From my daughter's laughter, you would have thought she was zooming down a ski slope.

Emily's next few adventures involve pushing all the snow off the front steps (while giving her watchful mom a casual wave), mounding up snow in the yard so she can leap into the pile, and making a snow angel.

As I watch my daughter, two words keep echoing through my mind: joy and delight. I can't help but see her pleasure in simply being out in the snow. Before my eyes, Emily has turned a common event into a wondrous experience.

I want my life to be filled with that same joy. Like Emily, I want to turn the ordinary into the extraordinary and turn a snowy yard into a winter wonderland of delightful adventures. As I watch my daughter, I begin to understand the reason Jesus tells us, "Any who will not receive the kingdom of God like a little child will never enter it" (Mark 10:15). There's a unique sense of joy and wonder in children that seems to be lost as they grow older.

I think Jesus wants us to remember the joy of being a child as we celebrate the gift of faith. I think Jesus wants us to recapture the delight and reclaim that sense of awe we had when we were young and thought of all that God has done for us. I think Jesus wants us to experience a little taste of heaven every day as we read God's Word and dine at His Table. That's what I want too.

Prayer: Heavenly Father, help me to recapture the wonder and faith of a child. In my Savior's name. Amen.

Reflection: What is one special memory God has given you from your childhood?

A righteous man cares for the needs of his animal.
(Proverbs 12:10)

UNEXPECTED VISITOR

As I go out the front door to the porch this afternoon, I'm surprised to see a Canada goose standing in the front yard. Its black feathers and feet contrast sharply with the whiteness of the world around it. With the snow and cold of winter, it's the wrong time of year for this bird to be in our part of the country. It's also unusual to see a single bird by itself—Canada geese mate for life and travel in pairs or with their families until they're older.

Yet in many ways this feels like an unexpected visit from an old friend. During the spring, summer, and fall, our yard is filled with Canada geese as they make our property their home during the warmer months. In the spring, we've seen goslings hatch and turn from small, mustard-colored bundles of fluff into leggy, chicken-size birds covered with downy gray feathers. These "yearlings" in turn transform into magnificent creatures with distinctive markings. Although we know these wild birds aren't our pets, we do feel a need to care for and protect them while they're here.

I miss the geese when they're gone during the winter. I miss watching the graceful picture they make as they float around the lake—the male goose in the lead, the goslings in the middle, and the female goose bringing up the rear. I miss the loud honk of their call as they warn away other birds or as they prepare to take flight. I miss their slow strut across the yard, which seems to indicate they have all the time in the world. Each spring, when warm winds again begin to blow, I turn my face to the sky and look forward to their return.

Because of the delight these creatures give me, I want to give back a little something in return and take care of this goose while it's here. I want to welcome it for this brief stop on what I know must be a longer journey. I disappear back into the house to get a few pieces of bread. Back outside, I tear my offering into pieces and throw the crumbs out to the bird. It gobbles them hungrily, then stares at me. I dust the crumbs off my hands, sit down on the porch steps, and stare back. "Welcome," I whisper, ready to enjoy our visit for however long it lasts.

When God blesses my life with such unexpected surprises, I've learned to take full advantage of them. This is one I'll enjoy for all it's worth.

Prayer: Heavenly Father, thank You for life's unexpected surprises that brighten my day and enrich my life. In Jesus' name. Amen.

Reflection: What is one unexpected way God has touched your life recently?

Trust in the Lord God always, for in the Lord Jehovah is your everlasting strength. (Isaiah 26:4 TLB)

COLD THERAPY

I land on the porch swing this afternoon with a bit more force than usual. Our family has been passing a cold around the last few weeks, and I'm the last one to catch it. What started as a sore throat has turned into a cough that has settled deep in my chest and left me physically drained. My body feels heavy, and I take every opportunity I can to sit—even if it's only for a minute. This time on the porch is a welcome rest.

I close my eyes and take a deep breath of the cold, damp winter air. I'm surprised to discover it feels better to my lungs than the warm air inside the house. As good as it is to sit here with my eyes closed, I don't keep them that way for long. I know if I do, I'll fall asleep in no time. I am tired down to my very bones from night after night spent nursing three children who have tossed and turned with high temperatures and uncontrollable coughing spells. Now that they're all recovering, I'm the one who has the cold and needs a nurse. Instead of getting the rest I need at night, I find myself trying to find a comfortable position that will allow me to sleep and breathe at the same time. I haven't been very successful.

For the past few mornings when I throw back the bed-covers, I wonder how I'll make it through the day. *Just put one foot in front of the other*, I think as I slide into my slippers and trudge downstairs to take care of breakfast. While my body moves at half-speed, my mind goes full-speed ahead with angry, complaining thoughts. *Lord, it's not fair that I'm sick. I have so much to do around the house and several writing deadlines to meet. Nothing stops when I'm not feeling well. No one takes over the housework and sends me to bed for a rest.*

How well I relate to the psalmist and his cry that "no one is concerned for me. ... no one cares for my life" (Psalm 142:4). Although I know my complaints aren't accurate—Tim and the children help as much as they can—it still feels good to vent my frustrations to God. In fact, "I pour out my complaint before Him; before Him I tell my trouble" (Psalm 142:2).

Today as I rest on the porch, I know it's time to start complaining less and praying more. I can pray for God's strength when mine is gone and for His patience when mine runs short. Mostly though, I can pray for His power to be made perfect in my weakness (2 Corinthians 12:9).

I take a deep breath to clear my mind, then bow my head to pray ... with my eyes open.

Prayer: Heavenly Father, I'm grateful that You give strength to the weary and increase the power of the weak (Isaiah 40:29). Forgive me for the times I dwell on my frustrations. Point me to Jesus' cross and empty grave as the ultimate means by which You overcame my weakness.

Help me to rely on You when my own strength is gone. In Jesus' name. Amen.

Reflection: What are your areas of weakness and how will you ask God to strengthen your reliance on Him?

There is a time for everything, and a season for every activity under heaven.
(Ecclesiastes 3:1)

THE FALLOW TIME

It's a dreary view from my porch swing this afternoon. Today is one of those ugly days of winter when the snow has melted to reveal patches of moldy leaves, muddy spots throughout the yard, and brown grass that lies flat and lifeless from the weight of the snow that has covered it. It's not like those winter days that arrive closer to springtime—days when the last snow of the year has melted to reveal tiny, green shoots pushing their way through the earth and holding promises of new life to come. Today there are no signs of growth. No budding developments. It is a fallow time—in my yard and in my life.

As I sit quietly on the swing, I admit that I'm not sure what has brought on this season of spiritual inactivity for me. I've tried to be faithful about praying and reading my Bible, but lately I don't spend the same amount of time on those things that I have in the past. Part of me wonders if this is a reaction to the many months I've spent trying to be a spiritual superwoman. Has my over-involvement at church—teaching Sunday school, leading two small groups, and missing worship to help out in the nursery when the need arises—led me to this point?

At this moment, God seems to be calling me to a place of quiet and waiting. "Come to Me, all you who are weary and burdened," He whispers in my heart, "and I will give you rest" (Matthew 11:28). I respond gratefully to the Lord's call, longing to be like Mary, who chose what is better and sat quietly at Jesus' feet.

As I linger here, I know the Holy Spirit is at work, cultivating the soil of my life and preparing it for the next cycle of growth to come. I know that "He who began a good work ... will carry it on to completion" (Philippians 1:6). Although today my life feels like the barren landscape of my yard, I am confident that with the Lord, even this fallow time will yield an abundance of fruit in His season.

Prayer: Heavenly Father, thank You for the generous way You care for me—enough to give Your Son to die for my sins, enough to send Your Holy Spirit to work in my life. In Jesus' name. Amen.

Reflection: Is your life at a "fallow time" or an "abundant time" right now?

He will send His angel before you. (Genesis 24:7)

SNOW ANGELS

The warmth of the sun's rays makes this cold winter day more bearable, though I have to shield my eyes from the brightness to see Emily playing in the yard. Clad in her snowsuit and boots, she is enjoying the afternoon. The fresh snow that has fallen has cleaned up the dirty, gray blanket that has covered the ground for too many days now. Besides rejuvenating the winter landscape, the new snow also has rejuvenated my spirits. I was tired of looking at the dinginess outside and welcome this new whiteness.

"Watch me!" Emily calls as she races from one part of the yard to another. Even in the cold, my heart warms as I watch my daughter. At each place, Emily falls backward into the snow, then moves her arms up and down and her legs in and out. Each time she gets up, an angel appears behind her in the snow. After a few minutes, it looks like the heavenly host is out in the yard with my daughter.

Seeing those wintry outlines reminds me of the prayer I say over my children every night, "Lord, send Your angels to guard and protect Micah, Steven, and Emily and keep them safe." It's a prayer I say to claim one of God's promises. Scripture tells me, "If you make the Most High your dwelling—even the LORD who is my refuge—then no harm will befall you, no disaster will come near your tent. For He will command His angels concerning you to guard you in all your ways" (Psalm 91:9–11).

God has guarded and protected my children. Our family has been blessed over the years to avoid serious injuries. Sure Tim and I have dealt with one broken bone (Micah's wrist) and more nosebleeds than I care to think about, but those things are minor—very minor. We have friends whose children are dealing with cancer, cystic fibrosis, severe ADHD, and more. We have other friends who have lost children to accident or illness. Our lives have never been touched in such a way, and for that Tim and I are grateful.

I know God's promise of His angels isn't a promise of blanket protection. The Lord doesn't guarantee us a life free of pain or illness. What He does promise is that He will be with us through whatever trials may come—and, for me, that is enough.

Still, today I'm thankful for the army that stands guard in the front yard with my daughter. Even long after the snow melts away, I trust real angels will be there—because God keeps His promises.

Prayer: Heavenly Father, thank You for keeping Your promise to send a Savior. Because You kept that promise, I know You also will keep Your promise to watch over me and my family. Thank You for giving us Your angels to protect us from harm. In Jesus' name. Amen.

Reflection: How has God recently protected you or someone you love?

As for God, His way is perfect. (2 Samuel 22:31)

RIDING DOUBLE

The side door to the kitchen bangs open, and Emily enters triumphantly. "Mom, come outside!" she demands. "I want to show you something!"

I hurry out the door after my daughter and stand at the top of the porch steps, hugging myself for warmth and wondering what I'll see.

"Watch this! Watch what Lauren and I can do!" Emily yells.

As I watch, Emily hurries over to the new training-wheel clad bicycle she got for Christmas. Her friend, Lauren, is already perched on the front tip of the bike seat, taking up as little room as possible. Emily starts to climb on the back. "Scoot over, Lauren!" she commands. "You're taking up too much room!"

"I'm not!" Lauren counters.

"I need more space!" Emily says, her voice rising.

Lauren, anxious to keep the peace, sighs and tries to move forward a tiny bit more. Apparently it's just enough to satisfy my hard-to-please daughter, who finally settles herself on the back of the seat.

Somehow, despite the bulky winter coats they wear and the fact that the bicycle is only made for one person, the girls manage to make room for each other. Emily starts peddling, and Lauren giggles over the fact that she is along for the ride. They travel a short way down the driveway together, then stop and get off. Apparently the two of them haven't mastered turning around yet.

I smile at the spirit of cooperation the girls displayed, but I also shake my head over my daughter's bossy behavior. She reminds me so much of myself.

I often see myself pedaling my way through life and forgetting there is someone riding along with me. Just as Emily only wanted Lauren to have the tiniest of spaces on her bicycle seat, sometimes I only give God the tiniest of spaces in my life. I become so set in my ways or so determined to do things how I want that I don't even think to ask God if He might have a better idea. Or if He'd like a little more room on the seat. Or even if He'd like to be the one to steer. Like Emily, I can hear myself practically shouting, "I need more space!" Except I'm shouting it not only at a friend, but at my heavenly Father.

Why don't I learn that when I grab the handlebars from God and only leave Him the smallest space on the bicycle seat—if I even leave Him any space at all—that I become like all the others who "turn to their own way, each [seeking] his own gain" (Isaiah 56:11). Besides the fact that I'm sinning, the direction my life goes in when I take control is usually the wrong one.

The psalmist tells me to "commit your way to the LORD" (Psalm 37:5). As Moses pleaded with God when he was leading the Israelites, my cry to my heavenly Father is the same: "Teach me Your ways so I may know You" (Exodus 33:13). Like Emily and Lauren, I ask God to turn my bike around. And as I climb back on, I scoot forward and make room—and give the handlebars to God.

Prayer: Heavenly Father, You want and know what is best for me. Forgive me for Jesus' sake for pushing You aside. Show me Your will and purpose for my life. In Jesus' name. Amen.

Reflection: How is God leading you to make room for Him in all areas of your life?

Be still, and know that I am God. (Psalm 46:10)

SoLITUDE

In the winter, our lake has a lonely feel.

Gone is the bustling activity of spring when the Canada geese arrive to reclaim the lake as their own and make a nest near the cattails in anticipation of the goslings that will arrive. Gone, too, is the continuous quacking of the ducks as they roam the yard all summer in their constant search for food. There are no frogs croaking, no crickets chirping, no wind rushing through the trees to spread a colorful tablecloth of leaves on the ground in one last invitation to play.

In the winter, the lake is still, silent, sleeping.

Yet even on days like this, I am drawn to my porch—my sanctuary. I settle on the swing and pull my coat up under my chin. I long to search out the warmth inside just as the geese have followed their instincts and searched out warmer climates, but I force myself to linger, to be still, to be part of the silence. It is in the silence that I often hear God speak.

Yet silence is not my natural desire. I flee it at times, afraid to hear God's voice, His message, His words to me. God's thoughts are not my thoughts and His ways are not my ways (Isaiah 55:8). I know when there's unconfessed sin in my life that I can be a willful child who puts her fingers in her ears and hums a lively tune so she doesn't have to hear her Father's loving reproach. Yet for all the noise I make, there's no drowning out the voice of God—no ignoring His call to repentance, His offer of forgiveness, and His gift of newness of life.

As I sit, I know this day isn't one for empty chatter about blessings I want and desired answers to prayer. This day I am still as the Holy Spirit opens my ears to God's Word.

Who can separate us from the love of God? I hear echoing in my mind. "No one," I whisper, remembering that "neither death nor life, neither angels nor demons, neither the present nor the future, nor any powers, neither height nor depth, nor anything else in all creation, will be able to separate us from the love of God that is in Christ Jesus our Lord" (Romans 8:38–39).

God's saving love and His grace-filled presence are constant in my life. Silence doesn't mean God is distant from me. It means I am distant from God ... and He will draw me back to Himself.

Prayer: Heavenly Father, some days my world feels dark and lonely, and You seem distant. During those times, point me to Jesus' cross and remind me that in His saving work You have drawn me to Your side forever. In my Savior's name. Amen.

Reflection: Reflect on a time when you felt distant from the Lord and recall how He drew You back to Himself.

This is what the LORD says: "Stand at the crossroads and look; ... ask where the good way is; and walk in it, and you will find rest for your souls."
(Jeremiah 6:16)

SUREF◦◦TED

Today the lake is half ice and half water as winter and spring wrestle for control of the temperature outside. The air is still frigid, but I notice that about a dozen brown ducks have arrived on the lake and are swimming merrily about. They are a sure sign that spring is not far off.

As the ducks approach the transition from the water to the ice, I am amazed at the effortless way they move onto the solid surface. With a quick jump, they are up on the ice and moving rapidly along. They don't slip and slide. They don't skid and stumble. The fact that they are so surefooted makes me shake my head in wonder.

Lord, I wish my walk with You were more like that, I think. *I wish I did a lot less stumbling and slipping and was more faithful to You.* Yet there are still times I find myself entangled in sin. This happens when I turn my gaze from Jesus and His saving work on my behalf. Before long I feel my feet stumble—then I fall. As I lie there flat on my face, I am grateful that God stands patiently ready to help me up. Far too often I forget that God tells me, "Let your eyes look straight ahead, fix your gaze directly before you. Make level paths for your feet and take only ways that are firm. Do not swerve to the right or the left; keep your foot from evil" (Proverbs 4:25–27). I also forget that it is He who makes the path level and keeps my foot from slipping (Psalm 121:3).

Each time I stumble—and each time my heavenly Father helps me to my feet again—I thank God for His merciful love and ask Him to send His Holy Spirit to guide me in the way I should go. I want to follow God's paths. I hold on to God's promise: "When you walk, your steps will not be hampered; when you run, you will not stumble" (Proverbs 4:12). With God, I am steady and surefooted.

Prayer: Heavenly Father, in Your grace and for Jesus' sake You extend Your hand of forgiveness to me when I fall into the snare of sin. Thank You for holding me tightly by the hand and for sending Your Spirit to guide me along Your path. In Jesus' name. Amen.

Reflection: What has caused you to stumble in your walk with the Lord? How has God helped you to overcome this obstacle?

*I will say of the LORD, "He is my refuge and my fortress,
my God, in whom I trust." (Psalm 91:2)*

COUNTING ON THE LORD

Winter weather in Cincinnati is unpredictable. One day the trees and ground are covered with ice from storms that blow in frigid temperatures along with a freezing mixture of rain and sleet. The next day, the red line on the thermometer climbs to the upper 60s, and TV weather forecasters warn of flooding in low-lying areas. Around here, I never count on having the same weather two days in a row.

In fact, this evening I'm enjoying another small taste of some warmer wintertime weather as I sit on the swing. Even with the sun starting its slow descent, the breeze that touches my face is almost balmy. But I know better than to become used to it. There is still too much of winter left, and tomorrow the forecast could call for snow.

While the variable winter weather usually only causes minor irritations—like having to keep a variety of medium- and heavy-weight clothing in the closet and having to deal with wintertime sniffles because my children haven't been wearing a warm enough jacket—I'm thankful other things in my life aren't quite so changeable.

Even with three children in the house and a variety of activities, our weekly schedule has a pattern to it. There are certain days for school and preschool, certain days for Scouts and other extracurricular activities, certain days for meetings (PTA for me, Scouts for Tim), certain days for entertaining, and certain days we keep the calendar clear. Dinner is almost always at 5:30 P.M., and at this time of year, the kids are all in bed between 8 and 9 P.M. Our schedule has a cadence to it, a rhythm almost. There aren't many surprises to be found—and I like it that way.

That's also the way I like my spiritual life. Although I know the world around me may be full of surprises—both good and bad—I also know my heavenly Father is described by words like steadfast, dependable, faithful, and trustworthy. These characteristics of God give me comfort and assurance that no matter how changeable the weather of my life may be, the Lord is unchangeable. I always can count on my heavenly Father. The Bible says that God's "faithfulness continues through all generations" (Psalm 119:90). It's a faithfulness that is best seen in the fulfilled promise of a Savior—a promise God kept with the birth of His Son. Now as a child of God, I hold to His promise of forgiveness and life eternal because of Jesus' saving work on the cross.

As I sit on the porch enjoying a warm breeze on a winter day, I'm glad that's a promise on which I can depend.

Prayer: Heavenly Father, amid all the changes that I face in life, I am continually grateful that Your love and mercy are changeless. Thank You that I can rely on Your Word and Your promises. In Jesus' name. Amen.

Reflection: What remains unchanged in your life and how does that remind you of God's unchanging love?

Let everything that has breath praise the LORD.
(Psalm 150:6)

WINTER'S BLESSINGS

In the chill of the evening, I sit on the swing with my coat pulled up to my chin. I've left behind the warmth of the house, and I can feel the cold creeping through the layers I've put on to protect me from winter's frigid touch. My breath creates clouds in front of me that quickly vanish as if they know better than to linger in the cold.

There is a certain slowness to the days and nights of winter—a slowness that is just perfect for sitting back to take a few moments to reflect on all the blessings this season has brought with it. I wrap my coat around me just a little tighter and remember simple things:

- The sight of the first snowflakes as they gaily dance to the earth.

- The delighted shouts of children ice-skating across the lake.

- The bright pink color of my children's cheeks after they've been outside playing.

- The sweetness of hot chocolate shared with someone I love.

- The smooth, white surface of freshly fallen snow that sparkles with the sun's light.

- The celebration of a new year—and the trials and blessings it will bring—with family and friends.

- The five-person snow family that occupied our front yard after the first real snowfall of the year.

- The warmth of our home after time spent out in the biting cold.

- The delicious smell of soup simmering on the stove.

- The glint of sunshine on the icicles that hang from the eaves.

- The lengthening rays of sunshine as night gives way to day.

- The white covering of snow that sparkles like diamonds as the sun's rays dance across it.

For me, winter is a time of warmth—the warm assurance of a home that protects us from the cold outside, the warmth of conversation and laughter from family time spent together, the warmth and assurance of God's love sent to earth in the form of a tiny baby to be my Savior. Soon the warmth of spring will arrive to herald a new season. Trees will bud, and flowers will bloom. While I look forward to that day, I thank and praise the Lord for His warm winter blessings that assure me of His faithful, saving love.

Prayer: Heavenly Father, when the night is dark and cold, thank You for the warm assurance that You are near. Your merciful love that sent Jesus as my Savior is the light in my darkest night. In Jesus' name. Amen.

Reflection: How have you experienced the warmth of God's love in simple ways this season?

Then you will go on your way in safety, and your foot will not stumble.
(Proverbs 3:23)

SKATING LESSON

Tonight the snow that falls looks like sparkling silver glitter being sprinkled from the sky as it floats past the spotlight that shines on the house. All around the yard, the trees lift their branches to catch the tiny flakes. The thin layer of white that covers them shows me they're succeeding.

Just this afternoon, Tim came into the house with a drill in his hand and proclaimed that the ice on the surface of the lake is six inches thick.

"Can we skate after dinner?" Micah asks. "We'll get our homework done right now."

"I'll be done in 10 minutes," Steven agrees as he heads for his books.

"Me too! Me too!" Emily exclaims.

So this evening our entire family dons their skates and heads to the lake. For me, this is the first time I've skated in more than 15 years. Actually, "skating" is a pretty generous word for what I'm doing—"wobbling around on the ice" is a better description. While I wobble, everyone around me gives advice.

"You don't need to lace your skates so tight," says Tim's

sister, Cathy, who has joined us for the evening. "They're already stiff because they're new."

So that's why I can hardly stand, I think.

"Don't let the front of your blades touch the ice. They'll catch and throw you off balance," Micah tells me as he skates swiftly by.

So that's why I keep lunging forward, I think as I lose my balance once again. It takes a lot of arm waving, but I don't fall down.

"Are you having fun?" Steven asks, zooming by. He's a natural at this and can't understand why I'm not flying around the lake at the same speed he is. *Not really,* I think, even though I smile in reply.

After lots of stumbling around and catching myself before I hit the ice, I take off my skates and head to the porch. It feels good to have my feet flat on the ground again. Besides, I know I'll enjoy the skating even more from up here.

From the peace and quiet of the porch, I watch as the crowd on the lake glides smoothly over the frozen surface. *Quite a contrast to me, aren't they, Lord?* I ask. My efforts at skating tonight remind me of my life as a Christian. Over and over again I find myself making my way across new territory—and it's often slippery going.

There are times I walk into a situation and feel myself flailing wildly, as Peter must have done as he sank into the lake when he tried to walk on the water to Jesus. Other times I fall flat on my face. But just as Jesus did with Peter, my Savior lifts me out of my sin and sets me back on my feet again.

One of my constant prayers comes directly from the psalms: "You are forgiving and good, O Lord, abounding in love to all who call to You. Hear my prayer, O LORD; listen to my cry for mercy. In the day of my trouble I will call to You, for You will answer me" (Psalm 86:5–7). While my walk with Christ may seem less slippery the longer I am with Him, I still stumble and fall. Although the circumstances of my life are always different, as are the temptations I face, one thing stays the same—God's willingness to pick me up when I fall, forgive me for Jesus' sake, and put me back on my feet again.

Prayer: Heavenly Father, You are gracious and merciful to me, a sinner. Thank You for forgiving me when I sin, for catching me when I fall, and for setting me on my feet again. In my Savior's name. Amen.

Reflection: How has God helped you to your feet lately?

Oh Lord, You are my light! You make my darkness bright.
(2 Samuel 22:29 TLB)

NORTH STAR

Tonight the sky is dark and clear as Tim and I come out to the porch for a breath of fresh air. "I should have brought a coat," I say. Spring is near, but the nighttime air is still cold. I move closer to Tim, who puts his arm around my shoulders for warmth.

As I gaze up at the sky, God's words from Scripture cross my mind: "Lift your eyes and look to the heavens: Who created all these? He who brings out the starry host one by one, and calls them each by name. Because of His great power and mighty strength, not one of them is missing" (Isaiah 40:26).

Standing here looking up into the vast universe, my heart swells with praise for the God of all creation.

Tim points skyward. "There's the Big Dipper," he says.

"And the North Star," I add.

Of all the stars in the nighttime sky, the Big Dipper always has been the one constellation that stands out the most to me. Each time my eyes sweep the vast blackness, this constellation's distinctive shape is easy to locate. Then just last year, Tim showed me how to follow the outline of the dipper down the handle, across the ladle, and back up to find Polaris—the North Star.

"People use the North Star as a reference point," Tim had explained. "They can do that because it always stays in the same place in the sky."

It's comforting for me to know that in a sky full of moving stars there is one that is fixed in place. If I lose my way, the North Star is there as a constant beacon, a steady light, a consistent guide—just like Jesus.

Throughout my life I have known Jesus as "the bright Morning Star" (Revelation 22:16) and the "light of the world" (John 8:12). He is my Savior from sin, the One who guides my path and lights my way. Because He is the fixed point in my life, I always know where to go when I need direction. Like the psalmist, I have only to ask, "Send forth Your light and Your truth, let them guide me" (Psalm 43:3).

Tonight as I look out into the multitude of stars that the Lord hung in the sky, I am thankful for the One He gave to save us, to guide our paths, and to light our world.

Prayer: Savior, in times of darkness we pray, "Lord Jesus Christ, direct our way unto You" (1 Thessalonians 3:11 KJV). Thank You for answering that prayer. Amen.

Reflection: How have you seen Jesus guiding your path and lighting your way in recent times?

SPRING

The Season of New Life

*The flowers are springing up and the time of the singing
of birds has come. Yes, spring is here.
(Song of Solomon 2:12 TLB)*

Give ear and come to Me; hear Me, that your soul may live.
(Isaiah 55:3a)

SPRING THAW

It's a wonderfully warm spring morning—the first warm day of the year—and I head out to the porch, ready to make up for lost time. There have been too many days recently when I've let other things interfere with this special time with the Lord.

During the winter, the cold often would surround me, driving me back inside before I could read more than a sentence or two from my Bible or begin to pray. Once I was back inside, I'd let life distract me from returning to my Bible. Other times, I'll admit, lack of motivation and my busy schedule kept me from picking up my Bible and heading out to the porch for my special time with God.

Now that spring has arrived, I sense that winter has left a coldness in my heart—a need to thaw out those places of indifference that have crept into my spiritual life these last few weeks. I haven't meant to ignore God, but that's exactly what I've done.

Today nature has spread a welcome mat of color and warmth. The grass is returning to its soft, green hue; the trees are beginning to bud; and I'm ready to reclaim my favorite spot. I've missed my time with God out here on the porch—the place where the very winds seem to carry His words. As I open my Bible, its thin pages flutter in the breeze. As I read, the coldness that seems to have gripped my heart recedes. In the warmth of the sunshine, I feel God's love. "Welcome back. I've missed you," He seems to whisper. *I've missed You too,* my heart responds.

Today, I am overwhelmed as I realize that my lack of faithfulness doesn't affect God's love and forgiveness for me. God is always faithful, always caring, always present. His merciful love is constant and perfect—extended to sinners when Christ died and rose for our salvation. The Lord's promise to me is that He will never leave me or forsake me (Hebrews 13:5), and it is a promise I cling to as I reflect on all the times I have forsaken Him.

When I neglect my time with the Lord, I miss out on all the blessings my heavenly Father has for me in His Word. I grieve over the time with God that I've missed over the last few weeks because it will never be regained. Yet I also know that God forgives me for those times I ignore Him— forgiveness that is mine because of the sacrifice of His Son, Jesus.

The swing moves gently, pushed by the warm spring breeze. I feel tears sting my eyes as I think of God's love and faithfulness to me. I look forward in joyful anticipation to many more days like this one—days when God and I will meet together in His Word so His Holy Spirit can do the work that needs to be done in my life. The sunshine of God's love is here today and always—and my heart melts at the warmth of that knowledge.

Prayer: Father, forgive me for Jesus' sake for the times I ignore You. Teach me to be faithful in my walk with You in the same way that You are faithful to me. May I learn from Christ's example and put You first in my life. In His name I pray. Amen.

Reflection: What areas of your life feel frozen and are in need of the warmth of God's love?

Behold I make all things new.
(Revelation 21:5 KJV)

NEW LIFE

Each morning this week I've watched a transformation that never fails to amaze me—winter is turning into spring. I've seen tiny buds appear on the straight brown sticks of tree limbs, and I know that in the next few days blossoms will follow—fragrant, white flowers on the pear trees and softer, pink ones on the crabapple. It's time for nature to put on its springtime best.

Around the porch I spy the purple tips of the hosta lilies; the feathery, dark-green leaves of coreopsis; and the folded, red shoots of astilbe all pushing their way up through the earth. A robin sits on the branch of the river birch. It cocks its head back and forth to survey its surroundings before flying away to share the news of springtime's arrival with others. From out in the yard, I hear more birds singing their songs of warm days, soft breezes, and new life. *Hallelujah,* I think, *springtime is here!*

As the swing gently moves, I realize that the fresh start of spring also applies to me. Because of Christ's sacrifice on the cross and His resurrection from the dead, I, too, can take part in this seasonal celebration of new life. In Christ, I am "a new creation; the old has gone, the new has come!"

(2 Corinthians 5:17). Through the presence of His Spirit, the Lord continues to work in my life and will be faithful to complete the work He has begun (Philippians 1:6).

I turn my face to the spring breeze, ready for what the Lord has for me in this new season. I want to be "made new in the attitude of [my mind]; and to put on the new self, created to be like God in true righteousness and holiness" (Ephesians 4:23–24). I know I can never accomplish this on my own. Instead, the Lord works through His Spirit to achieve this transformation in my life.

"Lord, I'm ready," I say softly, "for new roads to travel, new directions to follow, new insights into Your work in my heart. Above all, I am ready to experience springtime and the promise of new life in You."

Prayer: Heavenly Father, I lift my voice to sing a new song this spring—a song of praise and thanksgiving that You are always transforming my life through the work of Your Holy Spirit. In Jesus' name. Amen.

Reflection: What signs of new life is God revealing in you and around you today?

Thou shalt not go up and down as a talebearer.
(Leviticus 19:16 KJV)

TATTLETALE

The sunshine is warm, but the breeze is cool this morning. While the wind carries a robin or two across the yard, it also carries the soft, green smell of spring. In addition to the change in the weather, I can tell a new season has arrived by the sight of mallard ducks polka-dotting the lake. Our brown feathered friends have returned.

The front yard is bustling with activity—birds gathering the last crumbs of bread that were thrown out for the ducks, squirrels playing chase in the oak trees, mallards circling the lake. From the yard, I hear a robin spreading the news that springtime finally has arrived. I welcome the announcement.

The robin isn't the only one with a tale to tell. A single white duck hurries across the yard toward the others, quacking all the way. "Guess what! Guess what!" it seems to say, as if there is some interesting news to share. The other four crowd around in anticipation of the tale to come.

"You look like a bunch of old gossips," I say with a laugh. "What could be so interesting?"

Yet I know the lure an exciting piece of information

holds. I've both shared and received gossip, and I know the pain associated with both.

There have been times over the years when someone came to me with a bit of news that was just too good to keep to myself. Although I promised it would go no farther, I broke my word and lost a trust. There also have been times when words I'd shared in confidence came up in a conversation with someone who should never have heard them in the first place. I felt hurt, angry, and betrayed. *Never again,* I promised myself.

The Lord has lessons for me in both those instances. His Word tells me, "Keep that which is committed to thy trust" (1 Timothy 6:20 KJV). There are no provisions in that command that exclude really fascinating information or interesting gossip. There are no exemptions for those days when I'll be the center of attention if I just open my mouth and share what I know. There is nothing in God's Word that assures me gossip is okay.

My own experience confirms that. I've seen too many times over the years that "whoever repeats the matter separates close friends" (Proverbs 17:9). I've hurt those I love—and been hurt by them too—as a result of the sin of my lips. Not only are there immediate consequences to face when gossiping is found out, but Scripture says "that men will have to give account on the day of judgment for every careless word they have spoken" (Matthew 12:36). It gives me pause to know my words can have a lasting effect.

Today, as the tight circle of ducks continues to quack their news from one to the other, I ask God to forgive me for Jesus' sake for the tales I have passed along thought-lessly. I also ask Him to help me keep the confidences that are entrusted to me. On earth and in heaven, I want to be called a faithful friend.

Prayer: "May the words of my mouth and the meditation of my heart be pleasing in Your sight, O LORD, my Rock and my Redeemer" (Psalm 19:14). Amen.

Reflection: Has the Lord brought to your mind someone whose forgiveness you need to seek for betraying a confidence?

Create in me a pure heart.
(Psalm 51:10)

SPRING CLEANING

It's time for spring cleaning at my house. For the past few days, I've washed windows, cleaned walls, sorted through drawers, organized closets, and moved furniture to vacuum those hard-to-reach places that are so easily ignored. It's been a lot of work, but today I'm happy that part of my cleaning process is finished. I throw open the windows so the fresh, morning breeze can chase away the wintertime mustiness that lingers in the house. It's time to move outside.

The day is so warm it's hard to believe the last snow of the year only recently has melted. As I cross the yard, I'm amazed at the secrets that have been hidden beneath its surface—a pink mitten I thought Emily had lost, a hockey puck Steven received for his last birthday, a length of rope, a soda can, and bits of trash.

I grab a plastic bag and a rake from the storage shed and set to work. Within hours, the garbage is picked up, the leaves are raked out from under the bushes where they've spent the winter, and the dead stems of old perennials are trimmed to make way for the new growth. *Another job completed,* I think. I sigh with tiredness and satisfaction and sit down on the porch steps to survey my work. My efforts have paid off, and the yard looks wonderful. I roll my shoulders to relieve some of the soreness that has settled there, then head inside for my Bible. There's more spring cleaning left to do.

When I come back outside, I sit quietly on the swing for a few minutes as I let the Holy Spirit bring to mind those areas of my life in need of His touch. As we search through the secret places of my heart, I find there are many parts in need of the Spirit's cleansing work. Slowly and ashamedly, I unpack the prejudices and negative attitudes that have been stored for too long in the dark corners of my heart. I pull out memories of unkind words and heartless actions that I had dismissed at the time as unimportant. I realize now I never even sought forgiveness for them.

It's time to confess all those sins, to expose them to the light of God's truth, and to ask for the power of His forgiveness to flow through my life. "Forgive me, Father," I pray, knowing that by the very confession of my mouth my sins are no more (1 John 1:9). "Create in me a pure heart, O God," I continue, "and renew a steadfast spirit within me" (Psalm 51:10).

It is as if the breeze that blows through my house is also blowing through my heart. I am cleansed as God's Spirit works in my life. Because of God's gift of forgiveness, mine through the sacrifice of His Son, I know the newness of springtime has come into my heart.

Prayer: Heavenly Father, I know I don't have to wait for spring cleaning to bring my sins to You. I thank You for this special time of the year when I can focus on ridding my life of all that hinders me from trusting in You. Thank You for the generosity of Your forgiveness, which is always available to me for Jesus' sake. In His name I pray. Amen.

Reflection: What secret places in your heart are in need of the Spirit's cleansing work?

He put a new song in my mouth, a hymn of praise to our God.
(Psalm 40:3)

THE SONGS OF SPRING

During this season, one of the things I love most about my time on the porch is that each day I am surrounded by the songs of spring. Some days I hear spring's song in the rhythmic, drum-like beat of the rain on the roof. I've noticed the tempo of this piece can be either fast or slow, depending on the severity of the storm. Other days the song is found in the whistling of the wind as it blows across the porch and rustles the soft, new leaves forming on the trees. Still other days, the season's song is heard in the melodic trill of a brilliant, red cardinal that sits on a branch in a birch tree and shares a springtime melody with anyone who will listen. There even have been times during the past few weeks when the sound of the bells from a nearby church have mingled with the notes of the birds' songs. The music that results is heavenly.

Sitting here, I feel like I am hearing nature's response to God's command to "sing to the LORD, for He has done glorious things; let this be known to all the world" (Isaiah 12:5). For me, it is impossible not to join in that praise, even if it is only a silent song of joy that fills my heart.

It has been many years since the Lord "put a new song

in my mouth" (Psalm 40:3), yet the message and the melody are as sweet today as they were the first time I sang them. Through God's gift of His Son, I am not only a new creation in Christ (2 Corinthians 5:17), but I have been given a new song to sing to the Lord. Indeed, God's words tell me, "The LORD, the LORD, is my strength and my song; He has become my salvation" (Isaiah 12:2).

On this day of singing, I yearn to invite everyone I know to "glorify the LORD with me; let us exalt His name together" (Psalm 34:3). A song this life-changing is simply too beautiful and too important not to share. So I join with all of God's creation to sing to the Lord.

Prayer: Heavenly Father, through Baptism, You have made me Your child and put a new song in my mouth. May Your praise always be on my lips. In Jesus' name. Amen.

Reflection: What new song of praise, thanks, or adoration has the Lord given you to sing today?

"I have set My rainbow in the clouds." (Genesis 9:13)

GOD'S PROMISES

A steady rain hits the porch roof like the sound of pop-corn popping while I sit safe and dry on my swing. One of the blessings of this place is the feeling of being in a storm yet protected from it. It calls to my mind this image from Scripture: "He will cover you with His feathers, and under His wings you will find refuge" (Psalm 91:4). On my porch I feel sheltered under the wing of my Father's love.

I close my eyes and tilt my head back to let the soft mist of rain touch my face. The sound of the rain is quieter now, and I know the storm will be over soon. All too quickly the cloudburst ends, and I rise to go back inside. Yet as I look out over the lake, I see the Lord has one more blessing for me this morning. There in the sky is a colorful reminder of His promise of life to His creation—a rainbow.

I sit back down for a moment, reminded that the Lord's relationship with me is full of promises. Since His rainbow covenant that "never again will the waters become a flood to destroy all life" (Genesis 9:15), the Lord has given many promises to His people.

There is His promise of help: "I am the LORD, your God, who takes hold of your right hand and says to you, Do not fear; I will help you" (Isaiah 41:13).

There is His promise of compassion: " 'Though the mountains be shaken and the hills be removed, yet My unfailing love for you will not be shaken nor My covenant of peace be removed,' says the LORD, who has compassion on you" (Isaiah 54:10).

There is His promise of His abiding presence: "God has said, 'Never will I leave you; never will I forsake you'" (Hebrews 13:5).

There is His promise of forgiveness: "I will forgive their wickedness and will remember their sins no more" (Jeremiah 31:34).

Most important, there is His promise fulfilled of eternal, unconditional love and salvation provided through the sacrifice of His Son, Jesus. "For God so loved the world that He gave His one and only Son, that whoever believes in Him shall not perish but have eternal life" (John 3:16).

Of all God's words to me, this is the one I repeat most often—because it tells me that I am washed free of my sin and it decorates my life with beauty, love, and promise.

Even as the rainbow over the lake fades and disappears, I am assured that its promise remains—as do all of God's promises.

Prayer: Heavenly Father, I thank You that not one word has failed of all the good promises You gave (1 Kings 8:56). I thank You for being faithful in Your love and care for me. I thank You for the promise fulfilled of forgiveness and life eternal through the gift of Jesus. In His name. Amen.

Reflection: What promise from God will you repeat to yourself today?

"I am the light of the world. Whoever follows Me will never walk in darkness, but will have the light of life." (John 8:12)

WALK IN THE LIGHT

The sun is out this morning and blazing brightly after endless days spent behind gray clouds. Although I usually think of this season in terms of brilliant azure skies and beautiful pastel flowers—yellow daffodils, pink tulips, lavender hyacinths, and white crocuses—lately I've wondered when the colors and light were going to spring forth.

Today my wait is over, and I hurry outside to the porch to enjoy a few minutes of this beautiful day. As I sit in the sun, I'm reminded of God's call on my life to let my light shine. "You are the light of the world," Jesus tells me. "A city on a hill cannot be hidden. Neither do people light a lamp and put it under a bowl. Instead they put it on its stand, and it gives light to everyone in the house. In the same way, let your light shine before men, that they may see your good deeds and praise your Father in heaven" (Matthew 5:14–16).

Has my light been shining lately? I wonder. *Is it burning brightly?* I know this happens when the light of Christ shines through me. I know, too, this isn't something that happens because I want it to. It is accomplished only with God's help and through His strength. "Lord," I pray, "send forth Your light and Your truth: let them guide me" (Psalm 43:3).

But, Lord, what about those times when the way seems dark? I wonder. What about those times when I feel blind to Your light and don't know which way to go? Again I turn to God's promise from His Word, "I will lead the blind by ways they have not known, along unfamiliar paths I will guide them; I will turn the darkness into light before them and make the rough places smooth" (Isaiah 42:16).

Even through days that are dark with trouble or discouragement or trials, I know the Lord will lead me. Even on those days when the sun doesn't shine, the Holy Spirit helps me to walk in the Light.

Prayer: Heavenly Father, thank You for Your promise that I will never walk in darkness and that I will never walk alone. You have sent the Light of the world to walk with me. In Jesus' name. Amen.

Reflection: How has God's light recently helped you to walk through dark times?

"Let your light shine before men, that they may see your good deeds and praise your Father in heaven." (Matthew 5:16)

HERE I AM!

As I sit on the porch swing, I hear the distant call of Canada geese and wonder if they'll be touching down at our lake. My question is answered in a matter of moments. Amidst the honking that blasts through the air like a horn, a group of about a dozen geese glide across the water to a stop. Even after their arrival, the noise continues for quite a while.

Enough already, I think, ready to get back to my Bible and the quiet. *I can't concentrate.*

Who do they remind you of? my heart asks me.

No one, I answer a bit too quickly.

Think harder, my heart urges.

My mind goes back to some scenes from the previous weeks. First, there was that night at my writers' group when I couldn't wait to announce the stories I'd sold over the past month. Then there was the PTA meeting at my home when I drove my family crazy for days beforehand with my cleaning because everything had to look "just perfect." Then there was that conversation with a dear friend when I told about a "good deed" I was doing for someone—an action I had meant to keep to myself.

I'm just like those geese, I admit to myself. I like to announce my arrival with a flourish. I tend to let others know what I've accomplished. And, though I try not to, sometimes my good deeds are done for all to see.

But I know that isn't God's way at all. As a child I memorized the Bible passage that says: "But when you give to the needy, do not let your left hand know what your right hand is doing" (Matthew 6:3). I ask myself, *How much am I practicing that as an adult?* The answer has a sting to it.

The geese's calling starts again. I know from past experience they are signaling to one another that it's time to go. With a flurry of flapping wings and enough honking to sound like a traffic jam, the birds are gone as quickly as they came. Quiet settles on the lake once again—a quiet perfect for soul-searching and for asking God's help to work on a part of my life that needs changing.

Prayer: Heavenly Father, help me to get over my need for the world's approval. Remind me that my sense of worth and accomplishment come from who I am as Your dear child, one redeemed by Christ the crucified. May my desire be to please You in all I do. In Jesus' name. Amen.

Reflection: In what areas of your life do you seek to please others more than you seek to please God?

He was pierced for our transgressions, He was crushed for our iniquities; the punishment that brought us peace was upon Him, and by His wounds we are healed. (Isaiah 53:5)

FRIDAY MOURNING

Today Emily and I share my porch swing. She hands me the book she's chosen and snuggles next to me. I suppress a sigh. *Not this one again,* I think as I stare at the story we've read together so many times that Emily can recite it to me. Although I'd like to ask her to make another choice, I open the cover and begin reading the familiar words. From the transfixed expression on my daughter's face, I'd have thought she was hearing this for the first time.

When the story is finished, Emily hops down and announces that she's going to play in the yard. I put her book aside and pick up the Bible I carried outside with me. As I turn to the marker that holds my place, I am struck by the fact that, like Emily, I, too, am turning to an old, familiar story. It is the story of a sinless Man who wore a crown of thorns so I might one day wear the crown of eternal life. It is a story that starts with betrayal, includes political intrigue and rigged trials, moves to a hill with a wooden cross, pauses with a dying gasp, and ends in splendor—the splendor of a risen King.

Today, Good Friday, is full of the memory of the suffering Christ endured—the mocking, the thorns, the lashes, the nails, the cross. There is always the cross. A feeling of sadness washes over me as I read the events surrounding this day. I read of Judas' betrayal, Jesus' arrest, and of His trial before Pontius Pilate. Finally, with tears in my eyes, I read of His crucifixion.

I close my Bible and hug it to my chest. I know there is more to this story, but today I want to remember the suffering Christ endured for me. I want to remember a love so strong that it led my Savior to willingly give His life for me. I want to remember the sacrifice so the victory affirmed by the resurrection will be even sweeter.

On Good Friday, the day may feel dark and the sadness may feel overwhelming, but I will wait in hope. I know this story isn't finished.

Prayer: Lord Jesus, fix my eyes on You, the Author and Perfecter of my faith. Thank You for this story of sacrifice, redemption, and love. Amen.

Reflection: How does a day that focuses on Christ's sacrifice help you appreciate God's tremendous love for you?

It is good to wait quietly for the salvation of the LORD.
(Lamentations 3:26)

WAITING

My porch swing is the perfect place to spend some time today. This is a day of waiting. These 24 hours between Good Friday and Easter Sunday contain all the sadness of the day before but none of the joy of the day ahead. Today is a time of quiet reflection and stillness.

As the swing gently sways, I feel a sense of anticipation, an impatience to move on. I want to leave behind this time of expectancy. Like a child eagerly awaiting a special event, I want to see what tomorrow holds—to go forward into the celebration day. Later today I'll set the table for Easter dinner and arrange the flowers in preparation for the celebration to come. My sorrow at Christ's crucifixion is tempered by the fact that "I know that my Redeemer lives" (Job 19:25).

Jesus' disciples didn't have that assurance. Although Christ had promised that after three days He would rise from the dead (John 2:19, 21), the disciples weren't expecting a miracle. Instead they waited in secret and in sorrow as they worried for their own safety and grieved the loss of the One to whom they had dedicated their lives. I can imagine their fear and their questions. The breeze around me seems to carry those whispered worries, "What shall we do? Where shall we go? How did it all go wrong?" For Jesus' disciples there was no solace in the knowledge that their grief would be short-lived. On this day the rock still covered the opening to the tomb.

What if I didn't know the end to this story? I wonder. *Would my faith have been strong enough to go on?* That's a difficult question to answer.

There have been times when even a small bump in the road caused me to stumble in my walk with God. There have been other, more difficult, times when the Lord helped me to navigate a path full of pitfalls and hazards. My own faith-walk is as inconsistent as Jesus' disciples— seemingly rock solid one day and full of doubt and denial the next.

On this day before Easter, I rejoice in the privilege to wait in joy and not fear and to have the assurance of Christ's resurrection. I know how the story continues.

Prayer: Jesus, You took all my sins to the cross and endured suffering and death for me so I might have forgiveness and eternal life. I am overwhelmed to think one day I will live with You in heaven because the cross led to an empty tomb. Amen.

Reflection: What lessons have you learned from the cross as you wait for the joyful celebration of Easter?

"He is not here; He has risen!" (Luke 24:6)

EASTER JOY

There is a lightness to my heart and my step as I make my way to the swing. Today is Easter—the day Christ rose from the dead—and I am celebrating the miraculous ending to the greatest story ever told.

This morning at church I lifted my voice with hundreds of others to sing of victory over sin and triumph over death. At times my heart felt like it would burst from the jubilation it could not contain. While it is at Christmastime that I celebrate the coming of a baby who would save the world, it is at Easter that God's plan of salvation is fully revealed. Because of Christ's death on Good Friday and His resurrection on this day, eternity is mine.

The magnitude of God's gift of His Son, Jesus, and of Jesus' sacrifice are overwhelming. All my sins—past, present, and future—are forgiven. They have been taken to the cross with Jesus and will be remembered no more. I am a new creation in Him (2 Corinthians 5:17).

I open my Bible and read of the women who went to the tomb to find Jesus and instead found the stone rolled away. There they were told by an angel that Jesus had risen. I share their joy and amazement at this news, and I understand their desire to share what they've learned with others. As the women race to tell the disciples of Jesus' resurrection, my own mind races with thoughts of those to whom I might also communicate this good news.

As the Easter story continues, I witness Mary's meeting with Jesus in the garden. I can hardly imagine her joy as she realizes she is talking to the One she saw crucified. Here is her Teacher, her Savior, now risen from the dead. Like Mary, I proclaim that "I have seen the Lord!" (John 20:18) as I have witnessed the work of His Spirit in my life.

The story turns to Jesus' appearance to the Eleven. Like them, I look on His nail-scarred hands and feet and understand why their lingering doubts now vanish. This is, indeed, the risen Lord. I am humbled as I read His blessing of peace and His commission to go out into the world and teach and baptize others.

As Jesus ascends into heaven, I feel a mixture of sadness and joy. *Is the story over?* I wonder. I shut my Bible knowing the answer is an emphatic no. As I share with others the message of the manger, the cross, and the empty tomb—with God's promise of love and forgiveness for those who believe in Jesus—this greatest story ever told will continue to unfold.

Prayer: Father, from creation to the present, You have shown Your love to those You call Your own. I thank You and praise You for Christ crucified for me and for the glory of Easter and the triumph of my King. In Jesus' name. Amen.

Reflection: What Easter joy will you share with those around you this year?

God has said, "Never will I leave you; never will I forsake you."
(Hebrews 13:5)

A FATHER TO THE FATHERLESS

Dark, gray clouds bunch together in the sky as if daring the sun to try to break through. Just a glance at their swollen undersides tells me they are holding back heavy drops of rain—the same heavy drops that fill my eyes as I try not to cry. I feel raw with emotion and know it is only a matter of time before my tears will begin. Today, Easter's promise of new life feels distant.

I am always surprised at how grief sneaks up on me. Although my father died several years ago, there are still times when the pain of his death from cancer is as raw and fresh as the day it happened. This year my grief has been stirred by a part of the Passion story I usually skim—the part where Christ hangs on the cross and His Father turns His face away. Jesus' words have been echoing in my head for days now, "My God, My God, why have You forsaken Me?" (Matthew 27:46).

When my father died, I felt lost and forgotten. In the depths of my grief, I even twisted around those feelings of abandonment until they rested not only on my earthly father, but on my heavenly Father as well. *If my dad—who loved me so much—left me, how do I know God won't leave me too?* I thought. And in the moment of that question, I realized that was exactly how I felt—as if God had walked away from me when my father died.

It took me awhile to work through my feelings and to realize that God's promises are stronger than any emotion I might experience. He hadn't left me. Although I may feel alone, God's Word assures me of His presence. Through Christ's resurrection from the dead, I am also assured that one day I will have a joyful reunion with my father in heaven.

Today as my sadness resurfaces, I find myself going over this same story of loss again. *Lord, why are there times when my feelings deny what I know to be true?* I ask.

As always, God is infinitely patient. Today, I hold onto His Word. I grab hold of the first of God's promises that floats to the surface of my mind: "Never will I leave you; never will I forsake you" (Hebrews 13:5).

I know that, I tell myself.

"A father to the fatherless ... is God" (Psalm 68:5) comes to mind next.

Now I close my eyes and let the verses slowly sink in. "For the LORD your God is a merciful God; He will not abandon ... you" (Deuteronomy 4:31). I feel a hot, heavy drop escape from behind my closed lids. It falls on my clasped hands.

"For this God is our God for ever and ever" (Psalm 48:14).

I hear the rumble of thunder and the splattering of rain-drops. My tears fall as I acknowledge the many ways God shows Himself to be faithful in my life. The Lord is with me, and with a hand that is both gentle and firm, He continues to guide me.

Prayer: Heavenly Father, thank You for Your care and concern for those who grieve. Thank You for the promise of eternal life extended to all who believe in Jesus as their Savior from sin. Thank You that You comfort those who mourn. Thank You that You find me where I am and gently lead me onward. In Jesus' name. Amen.

Reflection: How does the Lord comfort you in your sorrow?

Lord, You have been our dwelling place throughout all generations.
(Psalm 90:1)

PORCHES

Even a month into the season, spring continues to announce its arrival with new growth and bright flowers. Throughout the yard, splashes of color appear against the deep green of the grass. There are tiny, white wildflowers scattered in the lawn, bright red buds on the azalea bushes, and soft purple phlox creeping over the wall of one of our flower beds. Soon the porch itself will be decorated with flower boxes full of colorful summer annuals. On a day like today, the grayness of winter is a distant memory.

As I sit here, a memory that isn't so distant is of other porches the Lord has given me over the years. When Tim and I were first married, our home was a small bi-level with a tiny, concrete stoop. Back then I'd sit on the hard steps for a few quiet moments alone with God. Yet when I was talking to the Lord, I never noticed the hardness.

From that place, God took us to a 150-acre horse farm owned by friends. At our first home there, our porch was a large deck built onto the back of a two-family house. Micah was born while we lived there, and I still remember wonderful playtimes out on the porch.

Next we moved to another house on the horse farm—a

blue cottage that sat at the end of a long, gravel drive. The house was surrounded by pastures and had a front porch with a swing. Micah and I spent countless hours out there, reading books and telling stories. Steven was born while we lived in that house, though we moved soon afterward.

At our next home we were back to a concrete stoop—though this one was a little larger than our first. I put a bench outside so Steven could join Micah and me in a special place that would help nurture the bonds between a young mother and her sons.

From there we moved to the home we live in today. Shortly after we moved in, Emily was born and our family was complete. In this home, our porch wraps around the house and is large enough to accommodate our family and friends—with room enough to welcome anyone who might walk by and want to join us.

What I love about all these porches is that each one has been a special place to nurture the bonds of a growing family. Each one has been a special place to share with those I love—and with the Lord. Especially with the Lord.

It's here on the porch that I pour out my heart to my heavenly Father and talk about the good and the bad things that are happening in my life. It's here God joins in my laughter and dries my tears. It's here I feel connected to the Lord in a way I do in no place other than church. While there are no limits to when and where the Lord can interact in my life, He is always close to me when I am on my porch.

In fact, one of the most valuable lessons I've learned on

my porch is that no physical place can be my sanctuary. Only God Himself is that. He is my "refuge and strength, an ever-present help in trouble" (Psalm 46:1). It is to Him I turn and in Him I trust. In the shelter of this porch I *feel* safe and secure. In the shelter of God's love, I *know* I am.

Prayer: God, I am grateful for the privilege of talking with You each day as I read Your Holy Word and speak with You in prayer. Thank You for this special place You have given us to meet. In Jesus' name. Amen.

Reflection: How does your special place help you to focus on the Lord?

Sow to yourselves in righteousness, reap in mercy; break up your fallow ground: for it is time to seek the LORD, till He come and rain righteousness upon you.
(Hosea 10:12 KJV)

APRIL SHOWERS

In the middle of a brilliantly sunny day, a large, gray cloud passes over the house. The air cools, and soon a hard, steady rain begins to fall. The drops hit the top of the lake, sending clear, round balls of water bouncing all over the surface. I watch from the shelter of the porch as the earth quickly soaks up this heaven-sent offering.

As suddenly as it started, the April shower is over. The daffodils again raise their golden trumpets to the sun while water overflows from the colorful tulip cups around the yard. Unlike the summer rains that simply wash the dust from the dry land, spring showers seem to replenish and rejuvenate the earth. They provide a welcome drink of water to the thirsty soil.

This quick April shower reminds me of two of the Lord's promises. The first is from Isaiah 55:1: "Come, all you who are thirsty, come to the waters." The second is from Revelation 7:16–17: "Never again will they thirst. ... For the Lamb at the center of the throne ... will lead them to springs of living water." These are the words that soak into my spirit when I need the living water that Christ provides—when I need a drink for my thirsty soul.

Often there are times when my cup is empty, times when I have poured out too much of myself without allowing God to fill me up again. It's then that I turn to the Lord and ask Him to rain down His mercy on my life and shower me with His love. Like the gracious Father He is, God answers my prayer "exceedingly abundantly above all that [I] ask or think" (Ephesians 3:20 KJV). He fills my cup full to overflowing with His forgiveness, love, and grace.

I am humbled by God's abundant provision for my life. I am humbled to know I serve a God who is "ready to pardon, gracious and merciful, slow to anger and of great kindness" (Nehemiah 9:17 KJV). In this season, as in every one, I am thankful to the Lord as His blessings rain down on me.

Prayer: Father, help me share with others the good gifts You give me—especially the good gift of saving faith in Jesus and the forgiveness He earned for me on the cross. Teach me to have a generous and giving spirit as I treat others with love, even as You shower me with Your merciful love. In Jesus' name. Amen.

Reflection: What blessings has the Lord recently rained down on you?

Above all, love each other deeply. (1 Peter 4:8)

ALLERGY SEASON

It happens every spring. About the time the bulbs push up through the earth and the flowering cherry tree in the side yard puts on its pink, springtime finery, Tim succumbs to the increased pollen counts of the season. His watering eyes, itchy nose, and pounding head send him to bed the moment he walks in the door from work. Unfortunately, allergy medicine doesn't do much good. Sleep does, and so Tim and I settle into a routine that will last for weeks.

After all these years of practice, I'm surprised that I'm not better at handling Tim's absence from our family life. Instead of graciously picking up the burden I know my husband doesn't have the strength to carry at the moment, I sit on the porch whining to God about my plight and feeling frustrated and resentful. *Lord, can't You just heal Tim so we can get on with our lives?* I ask.

As He does so often, God answers me directly from His Word. During my Bible reading tonight, I am stopped short by this verse: "Above all, love each other deeply" (1 Peter 4:8).

Isn't it just like the Lord to want to talk about love right now? I think.

Although I tell myself that I do love my husband, it's

that word "deeply" that snags my thoughts and won't allow me to continue reading. While I start each day by telling Tim that I love him, I know in my heart that this verse is talking about more than three words spoken more as a reminder to myself than as a term of endearment to my husband. Peter is talking about a kind of love that I'm not expressing in my marriage right now. It's unconditional love—the special love God showed when He sent His Son, Jesus, to earth to take my place on the cross and obtain for me forgiveness and eternal life. It's the kind of love that weathers minor annoyances—like allergy season—and major annoyances as well.

I've forgotten that from the beginning my marriage vows have been about commitment, not emotion. When I told Tim I would love him "in sickness and in health" that included allergy season.

I pick up my Bible and head inside to check on Tim and see if there's anything I can do to help him feel better. It's time to dig a little deeper into my love for him.

Prayer: Jesus, help me to pattern my love for others on the unconditional love You show toward me. Thank You for the tremendous sacrifice You made on the cross. Forgive me for the times I don't love others deeply. Amen.

Reflection: Whom will you ask the Lord to help you love more deeply?

Follow my example, as I follow the example of Christ.
(1 Corinthians 11:1)

Following His Example

Today has been one of those frustrating days when my children can't seem to get along. I close the front door on their shouts of, "Get out of my room!" and "Don't touch me!" and "Leave me alone!" and retreat to the porch to escape the commotion. My head spins as I sit on the swing and close my eyes. *How can they treat one another like that?* I ask myself. *It's like they don't love one another.*

Days like this make me feel that I've failed as a parent. It seems as though all my teaching, all my role-modeling, all my encouragement have been for nothing. *So this is my reward, God?* I ask.

I can almost hear the Lord's chuckle as I realize that I act the same way. As much as I hate to admit it, this same behavior is God's reward for all the effort He's put into my life. *How are you treating others?* He asks. *How loving have you been lately?*

I inwardly cringe as I see that my relationship with my children is like holding up a mirror to my relationship with my heavenly Father. Day after day I try to pattern my love, care, and concern for my children after God's love, care, and concern for me. While I think I'm doing pretty well, I often fail miserably. What I may not want to see is that when I am unloving or uncaring with my children, they reflect these same attitudes back to me. I easily acknowledge the good patterns and examples I choose to set for my children, but I want to close my eyes to the bad ones. While I'd like to pick and choose those parts of my life my children imitate, I know I can't do that. That isn't how life works. The Bible tells me that "a man reaps what he sows" (Galatians 6:7).

My own frustration and quick temper during the past few days have caused the temperamental outbursts from my children currently occurring upstairs. What they need is a new example to follow—one that reflects the higher calling we all have as God's children. After taking a few minutes to pray for God's help, I head inside to reflect to my children the love, forgiveness, and patience my heavenly Father shows to me.

Prayer: Heavenly Father, please help me to follow Your example of love and forgiveness as I interact with my children. Forgive me for Jesus' sake for the times I lose my patience with them. Help me to reflect You in all that I do and say with my children. In Jesus' name. Amen.

Reflection: What unloving areas in your life do you need to ask the Lord to help you work on?

I have [showed] you kindness, that ye will also [show] kindness.
(Joshua 2:12 KJV)

RIPPLES OF LOVE

From the porch I watch Micah take a few well-chosen stones and toss them into the lake. Each one hits the water with a satisfying splash, sending out round ripples that widen in ever-increasing circles. It intrigues me that a tiny stone can have such a big effect.

Kindness is like that, I think as I watch the growing circles. I know because today I was on the receiving end of kindness.

I spent the morning in the grocery store, trying to keep my eyes on my children and my shopping list at the same time. I wasn't having much success. Between rearranged store aisles and unnecessary items that kept mysteriously appearing in the cart, I was fighting a losing battle. I was frustrated from trying to hold my temper and my tongue at the same time. I wasn't sure how much longer I could hold on.

Lord, I feel like I'm failing at this, I prayed desperately while searching the cereal aisle for our favorites. *All I want is a little cooperation. All I want is to finish this job and go home. Is that too much to ask?*

As I stood there surrounded by my bickering brood, an

older woman pushed her cart past ours. Just a few feet away, she stopped and turned back to me. "You are a good mom," she said. "And those are beautiful children."

"Thank you," I stammered as I felt the kindness—and the truth—of her words pierce through my doubt and sink into my heart. I didn't know if this was a mom who remembered what it was like to shop with three active children or if it was simply someone who recognized the harried face of a mother in need of encouragement. Either way, her words were balm to my sagging spirit, and I was surprised how quickly they brought a change in my attitude. I felt relaxed, refreshed, and ready to get on with the day. Even my children reacted to my newfound calmness, and peace prevailed as we finished our shopping.

Now as I sit watching the ripples on the lake, I thank God for the woman whose few words changed my day from a burden to a blessing. I also ask the Lord to use me to start a widening circle of kindness that will touch the lives of others. I want to be a part of those ripples of love.

Prayer: Heavenly Father, Your Word tells me that "a word aptly spoken is like apples of gold in settings of silver" (Proverbs 25:11). Help me to choose my words carefully so they may be a blessing to others. Forgive me for Jesus' sake for the times my words hurt rather than help. In Jesus' name. Amen.

Reflection: What words of love and kindness can you share today that God can use to affect the lives of others?

You open Your hand and satisfy the desires of every living thing.
(Psalm 145:16)

KITE SEASON

The spring wind is at its playful best today. It comes up behind me with a gust, propelling me across the porch and hurrying me to my seat. As I turn the corner, I see that the swing also is being pushed by unseen hands. *Come sit,* the motion invites. *Enjoy the day!*

Out in the yard the wind lifts a few dried leaves into a circular dance before dropping them to the ground again. If all goes well, soon it also will lift the two kites that now dot the front yard like large springtime flowers. My children are busy knotting string and tying on tails in preparation for the trip aloft. It's fun to see teamwork in action as they work together to get their kites in the air.

In just minutes the job is finished. Steven stands with the spool of string while Micah moves about 15 feet away from him, holding the colorful kite.

"I'll count to three, then toss this into the air!" Micah calls into the wind.

Steven nods.

"One, two, three!" Micah yells as he sends the kite skyward. The string tightens as the wind scoops up the colorful piece of plastic held only by a line. Steven reels out string as fast as he can. The ascent begins.

"Look, Mom!" Steven calls as the kite climbs higher and higher.

"I see," I respond, leaning over the porch rail for a better view.

Micah takes the kite that Emily has been holding and runs to get it aloft. Soon it, too, is high in the sky, joining the first kite to sail on the wind like the first birds of spring.

I watch in delight as the kites dip and circle, climb and soar. Seeing them sail, I can't help but think of some of my dreams for my life—writing dreams, marriage dreams, parenting dreams—all of which have been given wings.

For a long time my dreams stayed earthbound, caught in a tangle of fear and pride that seemed impossible to unravel. I was afraid of failing and too proud to risk looking foolish to those around me. But the dreams persisted, and soon my desire to see them fulfilled exhibited itself in daily prayer. "Lord," I said, placing my dreams at His feet, "Thy will be done."

As I prayed, I waited, believing that God would do His best in my life, believing that my heavenly Father, who loved me enough to welcome me into His family through the sacrifice of His Son, would love me enough to answer this prayer in the way that was best for me. And He did.

While I was prepared for whatever answer the Lord gave, God opened His hand according to His perfect will and in His perfect time and gently lifted my dreams concerning my writing, my family, and my marriage and, with the breath of love, sent them sailing on high.

Prayer: Heavenly Father, I thank You and praise You for the wondrous ways You work in my life. I thank You especially for dreams come true. In all I attempt, may Your will be done. In Jesus' name. Amen.

Reflection: How has God given wings to one of your dreams?

*"Because he loves Me," says the LORD, "I will rescue him;
I will protect him, for he acknowledges My name." (Psalm 91:14)*

A Father's Love

From my porch swing I spy the pair of Canada geese who return to our lake every spring to nest. This year the female goose has decided to roost on top of a flat-roofed shed in the yard. The male stands guard on the ground below, close enough to watch over his mate and their nest and ready to protect them from harm.

When another pair of geese arrive, our male goose is quick to announce with loud honks and shrill squawks that this location is already taken. The new pair seem oblivious to the racket and ignore the warning to leave. I watch as our male goose flies into action, skimming across the lake to beat the outsiders with his strong wings and peck them with his sharp beak. It isn't long before the newcomers leave.

Over and over this week I've seen that the male's instinct to protect his family extends to anyone who ventures too near the nest. Our young neighbor, Jack, now takes the long way around the lake to get to our house. A few days ago he chose the shortcut by the shed and received some fierce blows from the goose's wings.

Although we try to steer clear of the nesting area, everyone in our family has been chased through the yard in the last few days. Just last night Emily came into the house crying that the goose had come after her. "I wasn't even close to him!" she said between sobs. I held her close, reminding her that we need to keep our distance. "He's just protecting his babies," I told her.

While the goose's encounter with Emily stirs up my maternal instincts, I understand his vigilance in watching over his mate and her eggs. I know, too, that his aggressiveness will continue long after the goslings hatch. Yet in this behavior I see a father's desire to protect his children. I also see a picture of the kind of protective love my Father has for me.

Over and over in Scripture, God is referred to as our refuge (Psalm 62:8), our fortress (Psalm 62:6), and our shelter (Psalm 61:3 KJV). He is the source of our salvation (Acts 4:12). In times of need I cry out to God as my protector. In times of distress I seek the safety of His gentle embrace. In times of fear I run to the sanctuary of His protective love. In need of forgiveness, I run to Jesus' cross. In all those times, God is there to protect me (Psalm 91:14).

I feel safe and loved knowing that God cares for me as He does. I feel even more loved as I consider that God's care extends to the gift of forgiveness and salvation in His Son, Jesus, who died in my place.

As I sit on the porch each day, I've found that God uses unlikely things and events to show His love for me. This week He used a goose and its mate to teach me about a Father's protective love.

Prayer: Heavenly Father, at all times, in all circumstances, You are my refuge and strength. You protect my way and provide shelter from the storms of life. You give me salvation through faith in Jesus. Thank You for the loving way You care for me. In Jesus' name. Amen.

Reflection: Reflect on an instance when you have seen God's protective love in your life.

Let your roots grow down deep into Him and draw up nourishment
from Him. See that you go on growing in the Lord,
and become strong and vigorous in the truth you were taught.
(Colossians 2:7 TLB)

GROWING ROOTS

This afternoon I gather my trowel and hand hoe, tear open a few bags of potting soil, line the top porch steps with the colorful trays of annuals I bought at the nursery around the corner, and pull on my gardening gloves. The threat of frost has passed, and it's time to plant the flower boxes that decorate my porch rails from May through September.

I grab the first rectangular box, which is still filled with lifeless vines and dried flower stalks, and begin to work. Usually each spring I just uproot the old plants and reuse the leftover soil. Last summer, though, I noticed that my flowers weren't as colorful as they had been in the past. The plants also took longer to establish themselves and didn't grow as large or as profusely as they had before. This year it's time for a fresh beginning.

As I empty the flower box into a waiting wheelbarrow, the contents slide out in one rectangular piece. The tightly bound roots hold the shape of the container. There was simply no room for new growth.

Placing the empty box on the steps, I refill it with dark, fresh soil. *Now for the fun part,* I think. I pick a tall, red geranium and place it in the center of the box. It's quickly surrounded by orange and yellow marigolds, pink and purple petunias, some white dusty miller, and a bit of trailing vinca vine. I stand back for a moment to admire my work and to imagine these flowers overflowing from the box by the end of June.

After I carry the flower box to its holder on the porch rail, I do one last thing—the hardest thing of all. With one last admiring glance, I pinch off all the flowers from the plants I've so carefully set in place. Now the box holds only green foliage.

"It has to be done," I say to myself, knowing that cutting back the first blooms helps establish the roots and give the plant strength. I know this is similar to how God works in my life.

Before God plants the fruit of His Spirit—"love, joy, peace, patience, kindness, goodness, faithfulness, gentleness, and self-control" (Galatians 5:22–23)—in my life, He tends the soil with love and care. Carefully and painstakingly, the Lord weeds out areas of sin and hard-heartedness so His fruit have the best conditions to take root and grow. Then, when the soil is ready, God plants.

I want the roots of God's fruit to grow strong and deep. As I read my Bible, attend worship, and dine at His Table, I know God is at work to fertilize the soil and bring forth new fruit in my life. By His grace, my "roots grow down into Him and draw up nourishment from Him"

(Colossians 2:7 TLB). God is continually tending the garden He has planted in my soul.

Prayer: Father, You are the Master Gardener who lovingly plants my life with abundant blessings. Thank You for the blessing of faith in Jesus and for the gentle way You tend my life's garden. In Jesus' name. Amen.

Reflection: What fruit is the Lord growing in your life right now?

I have learned to be content whatever the circumstances.
(Philippians 4:11)

THE COUNTDOWN

Although it's only mid-May, the countdown already has begun. Each morning as Micah and Steven leave for the bus stop, they grin and inform me how many days of school they have left. Each afternoon as they climb the porch steps, they give a loud cheer that their school day is over. Each evening at the dinner table, their conversation centers around sentences that start with, "I can't wait until ..." The boys' anticipation of summer vacation grows each day until it encompasses the entire family—me included. As I sit on the porch, waiting for the boys to arrive home from school, I mentally cross off another day from the calendar.

Even as that thought fades, another replaces it. Not just a thought, but a Scripture passage from my quiet time only moments ago. "I have learned the secret of being content in any and every situation" (Philippians 4:12). With a pang of guilt, I realize that I haven't learned that secret at all. While I know there's nothing wrong with looking forward to a future event, I also know I've spent far too much time lately anticipating the season to come and not enough time enjoying the season that's here. Although Micah and Steven led the battle cry, I quickly chimed in with my own over-eager anticipation of the days ahead when I could have been focusing on the moment at hand. It's time to ask God to change my perspective.

My eyes skim the yard to take in the beauty of this May afternoon. I am surrounded by colorful blossoms, a clear blue sky dotted with fluffy, white clouds, and more shades of green than I can count—yet I've seen none of it. My gaze was fixed on the future instead of enjoying the present the Lord has given me. *Slow down,* my heart says. *Enjoy today.*

I've warned my boys of the dangers of living in the future. "Don't wish time away," I admonish. In this moment of clarity, I realize it's time to take my own advice. I also know it's time to dispense a gentle reminder to my sons when they arrive home from school. The time is here to find contentment right where we are.

Prayer: Father, every hour of my life is a gift from You. Help me to live each day fully and not squander the time I have. In Jesus' name. Amen.

Reflection: In what areas of your life will you ask the Lord to help you enjoy the present instead of focusing on the future?

We are God's children.
(Romans 8:16)

A Child of the King

For days now, Emily has walked around wearing a white sequined dress, rhinestone tiara, and plastic, jeweled slippers. What's more, she tells everyone who stops to admire her outfit that she's a princess. I'm not sure if it's this new costume her dad bought for her or the fact that Tim always has called Emily "his little princess" that has her believing she's royalty. Either way, my daughter's new regal status has me out on the porch thinking about my royal lineage.

As the swing moves slowly back and forth, I think back to when I was a little girl. I don't remember my dad ever calling me his "princess," though I do remember other terms of endearment used in our house. It wasn't until years later that I learned I truly was a child of the King.

What amazed me when I realized the status my Baptism into Christ's death and resurrection had brought to me was that the "King" wasn't the ruler of some country. He wasn't a person who ruled in name but held no real power. No, this king was the "great King over all the earth" (Psalm 47:2), the "King of heaven" (Daniel 4:37), the "eternal King" (Jeremiah 10:10), and the "King of Kings"

(Revelation 19:16). In addition, this King was my heavenly Father who loved me enough to redeem me from my sins through the sacrifice of His Son, Jesus.

Because of my Baptism, I am now a member of God's family. "'I will be a Father to you, and you will be My sons and daughters', says the Lord Almighty" (2 Corinthians 6:18). How those words continue to amaze and delight me. Even today as I sit on the swing, I am overwhelmed at the privilege it is to call God "Abba." It is a privilege I enjoy because of God's merciful love, His gift of His Son, and His desire to make me His beloved child.

Prayer: Jesus, thank You for Your sacrifice—a sacrifice that made it possible for me to become a member of God's family, a child of the King. Amen.

Reflection: What does it mean to be part of God's royal family?

"Come with Me by yourselves to a quiet place."
(Mark 6:31)

MY QUIET PLACE

In the busyness that surrounds me, I feel God's call to simplify my life. Each time the phone rings with yet another request for my time, I ask, *Is this what God wants me to do right now?* To be honest, I'm not sure how to answer. I haven't spent enough time with the Lord recently to know the directions He might be leading me.

By putting in so many hours doing for others, I've pushed aside my time with the Lord. For days now the porch swing has hung empty, a silent reminder of what has always been a priority in my life—at least until recently. I feel out of touch with God because of the distance I've placed between the two of us. I feel like I've left the Lord waiting for me while I've gone on with my routine. I don't want to keep my heavenly Father waiting any longer.

I head out to the porch and sink gratefully onto the swing. As I sit, I feel a sense of peace—a peace that's been missing from my life. I've let my days get too complicated and let too many things come between me and the Lord. They've all been good things, to be sure, but not good enough to take time away from the best thing—my time with God.

I push my toe against the floor to start the swing's soothing motion. I ask God to help me get back to the basics and reestablish my priorities—especially the priority of this time on the porch with Him. It's during this time as I read His Word that God answers my questions, plants new dreams in my heart, and gives me the strength to get through each day. Meeting the Lord here has allowed me to better understand what Jesus meant when He invited His disciples to "come with Me by yourselves to a quiet place and get some rest" (Mark 6:31). This is my quiet place—one place where God does His work in me. A place where the Holy Spirit uses the Word to refresh my spirit and restore my soul. Amidst ringing phones and requests for my time, I've found the place I most want to be—here on the porch, resting in my Father's love.

Prayer: Father, it is a blessing and a privilege to have a special place to meet with You. Thank you for the quiet moments we spend together on my porch. Forgive me for Jesus' sake for the times I allow other things to interrupt our time together. In my Savior's name. Amen.

Reflection: Where do you go when you want to spend some quiet time with the Lord?

Make room for us in your hearts. (2 Corinthians 7:2)

MAKING ROOM

After a day spent cooped up indoors, the warmth of the evening draws me outside to the porch swing. The spring breeze greets me with a welcoming caress that carries the scent of rain-saturated ground.

The days are lengthening toward summer, and it's becoming harder to keep Micah and Steven inside after dinner to complete their homework. Tonight Tim is standing guard duty over the two grumbling prisoners who would rather be outside to enjoy the last bit of daylight. I savor this reprieve granted me from supper dishes and sweeping up and focus my thoughts on the peace and quiet that surrounds me.

Before long I hear the sound of the kitchen door opening and closing. I smile as I wonder if I'm about to be greeted by a prisoner making an escape. Instead, Tim rounds the corner of the porch. "They're finishing up their homework, and I'm finished with the kitchen," he tells me. "Emily is coloring, so I thought I'd join you."

I scoot over from my position in the middle of the swing to make room for my husband. As he sits down, he slips his hand into mine. We don't talk. We just enjoy the evening and each other's company.

Hardly a minute passes before I hear the sound of the kitchen door again. I look at Tim and smile. We both knew this was too good to last. *Who will it be this time?* I wonder.

Emily comes around the corner with her coloring book in hand. "Look what I did," she says, handing me the book as she climbs into Tim's lap. We ooh and aah in appreciation of the brilliant crayon marks that cover the page. "You did a great job," Tim tells her. Emily wriggles in delight.

As their conversation ends, I hear the kitchen door open and close again. This time it's Steven who appears. "Finished with your homework?" I ask.

He nods. "Can I sit with you too?"

I scoot closer to Tim to make room on the swing, and Steven hops on next to me. He leans his head against my arm and snuggles with me. I'm surprised he didn't grab his basketball and head for the hoop in the driveway, but I'm delighted he's chosen to spend a few minutes with us.

I hear the kitchen door open again. All four of our heads turn to watch for Micah. I see a look of surprise cross his face at the sight of all of us on the swing.

As Micah approaches the already-crowded seat, I see the question forming in his mind. *Is there room for me?*

Tim moves one way, and Steven and I move the other. It's tight, but we make a space in the middle. "Join us," I say.

As Micah squeezes in, I savor this moment of family togetherness. It's a vivid reminder of my blessings and of the fact that the Lord made room for me in a much larger family—His family. Because of my Baptism into Christ's death and resurrection, I know I am God's child (Romans 6:4; 8:16).

Tonight, as Tim, Micah, Steven, Emily, and I sit shoulder to shoulder on the swing, I thank the Lord for families and for the two wonderful families to which I belong.

Prayer: Father, I rejoice in the gift of faith and the blessing of Baptism, which has made me Your child. Thank You for making room in Your family for me. In Jesus' name. Amen.

Reflection: As you take time to enjoy the earthly family God has blessed you with, take time to rejoice in the fact that you are part of God's family.

"I go to prepare a place for you."
(John 14:2 KJV)

HEAVEN

This evening my perch is a rocking chair at the far end of the porch. From it I watch a small, brown sparrow build her nest above the front porch light. Several times now the bird has taken wing, then returned with a long, dried piece of grass or a small twig. With care and precision, she carefully adds the new material to her growing home.

The next time the bird flies away, I move across the porch to inspect her work more closely. Standing beneath the half-built nest, I spy familiar brown hair. Tim gave Micah and Steven their shorter, springtime haircuts on the porch only a few days ago to save on clean-up inside. I can see now that this nest has reaped the benefits of our outdoor barbershop. I also notice small pieces of colored paper and even several strands of green cellophane grass from this year's Easter baskets.

Watching the construction of this "home in progress" makes me thankful for the beautiful home Jesus has promised me. My Savior assures me, "In My Father's house are many mansions; if it were not so, I would have told you. I go to prepare a place for you" (John 14:2 KJV). While I know I can be content with much less than a "mansion," I also know the Bible describes heaven as having streets of gold, gates of pearl, and foundations of precious stones (Revelation 21:19–21). Out of love, my heavenly Father has created an eternal home whose beauty and majesty are beyond compare.

Yet for all its external beauty, what thrills me most about heaven is the knowledge that this will be a place of peace, security, and love. In heaven, "God shall wipe away all tears from their eyes; and there shall be no more death, neither sorrow, nor crying, neither shall there be any more pain: for the former things are passed away" (Revelation 21:4 KJV). In heaven I will spend eternity with the One who is "Alpha and Omega, the beginning and the end, the first and the last" (Revelation 22:13 KJV). Here I shall finally see my Lord and Savior face to face (Revelation 22:4).

As the sparrow returns to her nest once more, my heart thrills at the thought that one day heaven will be mine—a home for eternity built with hands of love. It is just one more gift from the God and Father who gives all good gifts to His children (James 1:17).

Prayer: Heavenly Father, it is overwhelming to think that because of the sacrifice of Your Son, Jesus, the glory of heaven will one day be mine. Thank You for Your generous provision for my life here on earth and for my life with You throughout eternity. In my Savior's name. Amen.

Reflection: What do you look forward to most in heaven?

Let everything that has breath praise the LORD.
(Psalm 150:6)

SPRING'S BLESSINGS

The sweet smell of flowers mingles with the fertile smell of newly turned earth to greet me as I settle on the swing. The warm breeze dances around me as if in celebration of the miraculous changes the earth has undergone in the last three months. There is a freshness to the air, a feeling of joy that the dark days of winter have been left far behind.

Lately the days have taken on a quickened pace because of end-of-school activities. I'm ready for the slower speed of summer. Amidst all there is to do this season, there is still time to take a few moments to think back over the blessings spring holds. Mostly I remember simple things:

- The feel of the first warm breeze that stirs the earth from the cold, deep sleep of winter.

- The brave sight of purple crocuses as they bloom against a winter-white blanket of snow.

- The first tinge of green across the landscape as the grass shrugs off its brown coat and dons a greener covering.

- The promise of rebirth as bulbs that have lain dormant all winter push up through the dirt to burst into colorful bloom.

- The cheerful sight of bright yellow daffodils trumpeting their welcome to the returning sun.

- The promise of seeds planted for a summer garden.

- The joyful sound of birds chirping.

- The soft rhythm of raindrops washing the earth clean.

- The welcome warmth of sunshine on my face.

- The rebirth in my spirit as I celebrate the resurrection of the One who is life itself.

- The shouts of my children as their kite catches the updraft and rises steadily in the wind.

- The colorful promise of a rainbow stretching across the sky after the rain.

For me, spring is a time of promise—the promise of rebirth as nature springs to life all around me, the promise of warmth and light as the days grow brighter and longer, the promise of new life in Christ as I celebrate His death and resurrection. This evening as I celebrate the miracle of spring, I turn my face toward the warmth of the sun and thank God for His many spring blessings.

Prayer: Heavenly Father, I thank You for spring and for all the promises it announces and fulfills. May the rebirth I see all around me extend into my life too. In Jesus' name. Amen.

Reflection: How have you experienced the promises of God in simple ways this season?

The Season of Light

Light is sweet, and it pleases the eyes to see the sun.
(Ecclesiastes 11:7)

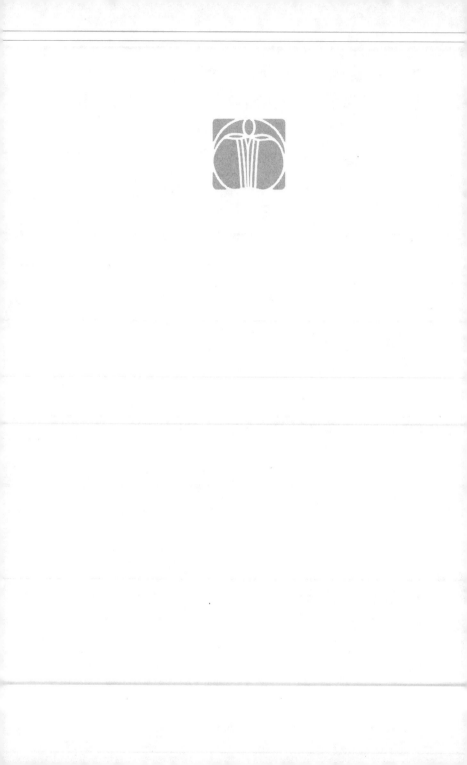

Children are an heritage of the LORD. (Psalm 127:3 KJV)

OUR GIFTS FROM GOD

This morning the sun beckons the children and me outside with its rays of beginning-of-the-summer warmth. We take a walk around the lake, feed the ducks, then take turns pushing one another on the wooden swing that hangs from the big oak tree in our side yard. After awhile, I retreat to the porch swing and watch the boys push Emily.

"Hang on tight!" Micah warns.

"Don't let go!" Steven reminds her.

Emily's giggles of delight let them know she appreciates the attention she's receiving and that her grip is tighter than either of them may believe.

I sit in wonder and amazement as I watch these three gifts God has given to Tim and me. First is Micah, tall and lean and beginning to push away from the restraints of his mother's love. Then there's Steven, compact and muscular and full of affection. Last is Emily, pretty and petite and full of wonder at a world that is ever new.

Although these three share the brown hair, round face, and distinctive features that proclaim them to be siblings, they are all so different—each one uniquely created by God.

I'm discovering that raising children is the ultimate of God's unexpected surprises. First came the nine months of anticipation as Tim and I awaited each baby's arrival. Now with three children, there are days upon days of new challenges, new frustrations, new adventures, new joys, and new sorrows as we work together to raise Micah, Steven, and Emily in a Godly manner. For me, parenting is a journey of events and emotions that often leaves me wondering what's around the next bend in the road.

I know for certain, though, that this road I travel as I raise my children is one I do not walk alone. Amid our joy, Tim and I trust in God's presence as He encourages our parenting efforts and shares our happiness. God has been with us in times of sorrow as well. His promise to us is "when you pass through the waters, I will be with you; and when you pass through the rivers they will not sweep over you" (Isaiah 43:2). God's strength has been our strength when we've encountered situations and dilemmas too difficult to face alone. He is there with forgiveness for Jesus' sake when we make mistakes, and He picks us up and sets us back on the right path.

Even when the road we walk in raising our children isn't smooth and straight, we can be assured God is with us. He goes before us to be our Light and our Guide.

Prayer: Lord and Giver of Life, help us to raise our children in a way that brings honor to You. With the help of Your Holy Spirit, guide us through Your Word to make wise decisions as we raise these children You have entrusted to our care. In Jesus' name. Amen.

Reflection: How will God help you care for your children at this point in their lives?

"All men will know that you are My disciples, if you love one another."
(John 13:35)

MARKINGS

Since early spring I have watched six goslings grow up before my eyes. Back in April I spotted the fuzzy, mustard-colored babies scurrying across the yard between their mother and father. I called Tim, Micah, Steven, and Emily out to the porch. "The goslings have arrived!" I announced.

We all gazed with delight as the babies hopped into the lake to trail behind their father for their first swim. The female goose followed the babies, her head up and her eyes bright as she kept alert for signs of danger. My family watched from the porch, welcoming these new neighbors who would share our lake for months to come.

As the weeks passed, the goslings grew from four or five inches in height to more than a foot tall. Although they remained close to mom and dad for protection, they began to venture farther away with each passing day. The goslings were growing up.

Now that it's June, I see that the goslings' soft, gray color is giving way to the distinctive black, white, and gray feathers of an adult Canada goose. There is no doubt now what kind of birds these are. At last the baby geese have their markings.

As a Christian, what are my markings? I ask myself as I watch the young birds move even farther from the safe circle the adult geese have provided. *What is it that distinguishes me from someone who doesn't believe in Jesus as Lord and Savior?*

The first thing that comes to my mind is a Scripture verse, "A new command I give you: Love one another. As I have loved you, so you must love one another. By this all men will know that you are My disciples, if you love one another" (John 13:34–35).

In that moment, I realize it is when I reach out to those around me with love—a love prompted by the working of the Holy Spirit—that others will see Christ in me. I can show love through the quiet comfort of a hug for someone who is hurting, through words of encouragement to someone who feels depressed or unworthy, through a helping hand to someone in need. When I show love because of the love God first showed to me when He gave His Son to die on a cross and rise from the dead, I show the world I am one of God's own, a follower of Jesus, a Christian.

Prayer: Lord, I want to bear the markings of Your disciple. Help me to live a life of love that overflows from the love You showed me through the awesome gift of salvation. In Your name I pray. Amen.

Reflection: What doors has God opened in your life that you might show His love to those around you and distinguish yourself as a follower of Jesus Christ?

Follow the way of love. (1 Corinthians 14:1)

LESSON OF LOVE

Out in the front yard, Micah stands at the edge of the lake with his fishing pole in hand. I watch as he chooses a worm from his container and patiently baits his hook. I know he's waited all morning for this moment, and I can imagine his delight at finally being outside and about to make his first cast of the day. At breakfast he told me he was "going to catch a big one." Now his moment has finally arrived. I hope the fish are biting.

Out of the corner of my eye I see Emily wandering aimlessly among the oak trees in the side yard. As she passes the rope swing, she gives it a twirl and a look of longing. I know that soon she'll head my way to ask if I'll give her a push.

Instead of coming to me, Emily approaches her brother. Although I'm too far away to hear her request, I know what it is. "Micah, will you push me?"

I expect my son to shake his head and tell her to "get lost" as he's done so many times in the past. After all, he's been looking forward to fishing all morning. I don't know that I'd blame him for turning her down. To my surprise, Micah carefully puts down his pole and follows Emily to the swing.

The look on my daughter's face is pure joy as her brother helps her onto the flat piece of wood and tells her to hold on tightly. "Higher, Micah, higher!" she shouts as he begins pushing. Minutes pass as Emily goes back and forth through the air.

When she finally slows down, Micah adds an extra treat. He winds the swing up tightly until Emily is scrunched over on the seat between a tight triangle of rope. "One, two, three!" Micah calls. As he releases the rope, Emily twirls around and around. Her laughter twirls with her.

When the swing finally stills, Emily climbs off and dizzily follows her brother back to the lake and his waiting fishing pole. She sits down in the grass by him, content to let him return to his fun.

"Lord, did You see that?" I ask out loud, amazed at the love I've just seen in action. Although I've taught my children how they should behave, I'm still a bit taken aback when they remember what I've taught them—especially when they remember in such a kind and loving way.

I hold Jesus' sacrificial love up to my children as the ultimate illustration of true love. His death on the cross to give us forgiveness for our sins is an amazing gift to an unworthy world. Yet it's a gift He freely gave.

"Love one another," He asks of us today. "As I have loved you, so you must love one another" (John 13:34). This morning, in my front yard, I saw an example of the kind of love Jesus meant. The kind of love that puts aside personal wants and does something for someone else. The kind of love that says, "You go first. I can wait." The kind of love that sacrifices its desires for someone else.

This morning I graduated from teacher to student as my son taught me a lesson of love.

Prayer: Heavenly Father, of all the lessons I've learned in life the most life-changing is the lesson of love taught by Your Son. Thank You for His sacrifice for me. Thank You for the gift of faith to believe in Jesus as my Savior. Help me to share His love with those around me. In Jesus' name. Amen.

Reflection: How has God recently shown you love in action?

Taste and see that the LORD is good.
(Psalm 34:8)

PORCH PICNIC.

Heading to the porch with bologna sandwiches, potato chips, apples, and drinks is Steven's idea. "Mom, can we eat lunch outside?" he asks as I open the refrigerator to prepare our midday meal.

"Sure," I reply. "You get a bag of chips from the pantry, and I'll make the sandwiches. Micah, you're in charge of drinks, and Emily can get some napkins."

We complete our tasks quickly and head out into the warm summer sunshine carrying paper plates laden with food. "Do you want to eat out on the dock or under a tree?" I ask Steven as I head down the porch steps and into the yard. "I'll go back in for the blanket."

"I want to eat right here," he says, settling down on the porch steps.

My son's choice surprises me. I had thought in terms of a more traditional picnic when he had asked if we could eat outside.

"Then right here it is," I say, sitting down next to him. Micah and Emily settle in too. Soon the porch is filled with the sound of contented munching and silly knock-knock jokes—my children's favorite.

"Knock knock," Steven starts.

"Who's there?" we chorus.

"Pencil."

"Pencil who?"

"Pencil fall down if you don't wear a belt!"

The sound of groans and giggles bounces off the porch ceiling and drifts out into the yard to be shared with the ducks that stand by hoping for a handout. *What a picture we make,* I think as I look around our "feasting table" into the faces of my children. I know without a doubt that this is the stuff sweet memories are made of. I know, too, that it is all a gift from God, who gives to His children in abundance.

When I think of God's gifts in terms of a feast, I imagine a table laden with food that will tantalize my taste buds and nourish my spirit. My thoughts include our home and family, our clothes and food, our bodies and minds, in addition to the many blessings God grants me daily.

God also has provided a real Table where I dine on heavenly food. My Host doesn't even ask me to put on my finest clothes to share in the honor of dining with Him. When I arrive at the feast, I don't have to hide the fact that my clothes may be dirty or torn—or that my life is dirty and torn as well. I go before the Lord of this banquet with all my weaknesses, failures, and imperfections in plain view, knowing that as I eat this bread and drink this wine I am receiving His body and blood, which gives me forgiveness for my sins and strength for the days ahead.

As lunch ends and we begin cleaning up our mess, I say

a silent prayer of wonder and thanksgiving to the One who seasons my life with goodness and grace and provides numerous opportunities to taste and see that the Lord is good (Psalm 34:8).

Prayer: Jesus, You are the true bread of life. You are everything I need. Thank You for the opportunity to be strengthened through participation in Your Supper. Thank You for providing so generously for my life. Amen.

Reflection: How has the Lord shown you recently that you can, indeed, taste and see that He is good?

Not one word has failed of all the good promises He gave.
(1 Kings 8:56)

A PROMISE KEPT

I hear the kitchen door slam and listen to the sound of footsteps running across the wooden porch floor. Just minutes ago I had grabbed my Bible and slipped outside for some time by myself. Now, though, it seems my time is up. My children have found me.

Micah, Steven, and Emily round the corner of the porch and head in my direction. While Emily climbs onto the swing, the boys stand in front of me.

"Are you having your quiet time with God?" Emily asks.

"I was just about to," I say, shutting my Bible. "What can I do for all of you?"

"You said you would watch us swim after lunch," Micah answers.

"You promised," Steven adds.

"We're hot. We want to go now," Emily pipes in.

As much as I'd like this quiet moment alone to continue, I did make a promise to my children. Being faithful to my word to my children is a reflection of God's faithfulness in keeping His Word to me, His child.

Many times I've taken out my Bible and shown God's promises to Micah, Steven, and Emily. We've searched the

Scriptures together and discovered that God promised to send a Savior: "I will put enmity between you and the woman, and between your offspring and hers; he will crush your head, and you will strike his heel" (Genesis 3:15). We have found that Jesus pledged His peace: "Peace I leave with you; My peace I give you" (John 14:27). We've found Christ's commitment of His presence in our lives: "And surely I am with you always, to the very end of the age" (Matthew 28:20). And we've been reassured by Jesus' promise of the Holy Spirit to be our Comforter and our Guide: "And I will ask the Father, and He will give you another Counselor to be with you forever ... the Holy Spirit, whom the Father will send in My name, will teach you all things and will remind you of everything I have said to you" (John 14:16, 26).

I don't want to ignore the promises I've made to my children any more than I want my heavenly Father to ignore the promises He's made to me. I mark my place, and I put my Bible down on the swing. I'll keep it out until I can return later in the day for my quiet time with God. Now, I have two promises to keep.

Prayer: Heavenly Father, Your faithfulness to Your promises shines forth into the lives of Your children. Help me also to keep the promises I make. May my faithfulness reflect Your perfect faithfulness to those around me. In Jesus' name. Amen.

Reflection: Think of the promises you've made recently. Have you been faithful in keeping them?

*Delight yourself in the LORD, and He will give you
the desires of your heart. (Psalm 37:4)*

MY HEART'S DESIRE

As I head out to the porch and into the early afternoon heat of the July sun, I pick up the bag of sweet corn lying on the kitchen counter. Our Fourth of July celebration is coming up, and I have a lot to do in preparation.

I pull the first ear of corn from the bag and begin shucking. A breeze stirs, lifting the red, white, and blue bunting that hangs from the porch rails and fluttering the flags that fly from either end of the porch. Our home is decked out in its patriotic best. As I work, I am suddenly struck with a thought so wonderful it takes my breath away. "Lord," I whisper, "I am living a moment I've dreamed about for as long as I can remember."

Even as a little girl, I would see pictures of houses with front porches and flags flying, and something would stir deep within me. *Wouldn't it be wonderful some day ...* I'd dream, afraid to voice the thought out loud for fear the telling would somehow make the dream unattainable.

Yet today, here I sit ... on my own front porch, shucking corn for my own Fourth of July celebration, with flags flying around me. I feel like part of a Norman Rockwell painting, and I absolutely love every moment of it. I sit quietly for a few minutes as I take all this in. God has given me my heart's desire.

As I pick up another ear of corn and begin to work again, a verse comes to mind, "Every good and perfect gift is from above, coming down from the Father of the heavenly lights" (James 1:17).

Thank You, God! my heart shouts. *Thank You for every good and perfect gift that You have given me.*

As that verse winds its way through my thoughts, so does a list of all the things I have for which to be thankful. It begins with my faith, my family, my friends, and, especially on this day, includes the freedom enjoyed in our country. The list shows me that my life is abundantly blessed, and I am touched by this knowledge down to my very soul. My list shows me something else as it comes around to end right where it began. My list is a perfect circle that begins and ends with God's greatest gift—Jesus. In the light of His presence, all other gifts pale. He is truly my heart's desire.

Prayer: God of all good things, I praise and thank You for the many delightful ways You touch my life. Through all You do and all You give, You show me that You are a Father who loves and cares for His children. In my Savior's name. Amen.

Reflection: What desires of your heart has the Lord given to you?

"Can anyone hide in secret places so that I cannot see him?"
declares the LORD. (Jeremiah 23:24)

HIDE AND SEEK

I can't help but smile as I watch the game of hide-and-seek going on in the yard around me. Micah and Steven and two friends have been taking turns hiding behind trees and bushes or among the tall, dry patches of maiden grass that line one part of the yard. This time, though, one of the boys, Josiah, has hidden under the front porch steps. I can hear his snickers of delight as he realizes he's found a place to hide that no one has thought of yet. I smile along with him.

It's Micah's turn to be It, and he quickly finds the other two boys behind some trees. Instead of searching for the last missing player, though, he's distracted by the arrival of a new friend. After a brief conversation, those four boys hurry off to the backyard to start another game. I open my mouth to say something, but close it again. I wonder how long it will take for Josiah to emerge.

A few more minutes pass before Josiah crawls out. My smile fades when I see the confused look on his face. *How could they have forgotten me?* the look says. Josiah searches the yard with his eyes, wondering where everyone is. "They're around back," I tell him.

"Thanks," he mutters.

As he turns the corner of the house to enter the backyard, I hear him shout, "Hey, guys, you forgot me!" I hear shouts of laughter, and, happily, I hear Josiah join in. I can smile again too.

Watching the boys' game has made me doubly thankful. First, I am thankful that the Lord never hides from me. When I seek Him, He is there. He is always available to hear my prayers, impart forgiveness, strengthen my faith, comfort my suffering, and share my joy. He tells me, "I am with you and will watch over you wherever you go, ... I will not leave you" (Genesis 28:15).

Second, I am thankful that when I am lost, God searches for me. Like the good shepherd that He is, the Lord seeks out any of His sheep that have gone astray. Jesus told His followers, "Suppose one of you has a hundred sheep and loses one of them. Does he not leave the ninety-nine in the open country and go after the lost sheep until he finds it? And when he finds it, he joyfully puts it on his shoulder and goes home" (Luke 15:4–6).

The Lord never hides from His children, and He doesn't forget us or leave us in our hiding places—He seeks us out because He desires for the lost to be found.

Prayer: Heavenly Father, not only do You search me and know me, but You search for me when I am lost. Through Jesus' saving action on the cross and the waters of Baptism, You have made me Yours forever. Your care and merciful love for me are overwhelming! In Jesus' name. Amen.

Reflection: Have you been hiding from God? How is God seeking you out right now?

Praise be to the God and Father of our Lord Jesus Christ,
the Father of compassion and the God of all comfort, who comforts us
in all our troubles, so that we can comfort those in any trouble with the comfort
we ourselves have received from God. (2 Corinthians 1:3–4)

GOD'S COMFORT

Micah, Steven, and Emily have dragged the garden hose and sprinkler into the front yard and are chasing one another through the cold spray of water. It's the perfect prescription for the oppressive heat of the afternoon.

Suddenly the shouts of laughter stop, and I can see the confusion on Emily's face. "What happened to the water?" she asks. The boys pretend innocence, even though I see Steven standing off to the side, crimping the hose to stop the flow of water. "You had better check the sprinkler, Emily," Micah prompts. As Emily leans down to see what could be causing the problem, I open my mouth to warn her—but I'm too late. Steven releases the hose, and the water shoots up into my daughter's face.

I see a kaleidoscope of emotions cross Emily's face— first bewilderment, then hurt, then anger. "Micah and Steven, you got it in my eyes!" she screams as she heads toward me on the porch. Emily's tears are flowing freely as I gather my dripping daughter into my arms and pull her onto my lap. I hug her close and kiss away her tears. "You'll be okay," I soothe. "I'm here. I have you."

After a minute or two her sobs lessen, and she relaxes against me.

Although I try to have a positive perspective on life, like Emily I've found that not all of life's unexpected surprises are fun. There have been times when it feels as though life has hit me in the face like water streaming from the hose. When that happens, I come up bewildered, hurt, and angry.

Dealing with the threat of cystic fibrosis with our oldest child was one of those unexpected surprises. When Micah was 9 months old, his weight began dropping. As the weeks passed with no improvement, Tim and I took him to the pediatrician to see if the cause could be determined. The words "cystic fibrosis" were mentioned early in the conversation, and testing was started. *Please, Lord, not that,* I prayed through tears.

Through His Word, God reassured me, "I have heard your prayer and seen your tears" (2 Kings 20:5). In my despair, God was my comfort. He was there amid everything I was going through, and I clung to His promise that He would be with me always (Matthew 28:20).

Beyond His presence, the Lord sent my friends to be His hands and feet. They waited with us for Micah's diagnosis with prayers, kind words, and warm hugs. Each one of them faithfully followed God's command to "be sympathetic, love as brothers, be compassionate" (1 Peter 3:8). They offered strong shoulders, attentive ears, caring hearts, and loving embraces. Each of these things was exactly what I needed.

When the tests were completed, we found that Micah didn't have cystic fibrosis. Instead, the doctors diagnosed an ongoing case of diarrhea as the cause of his weight loss. A few weeks of medication and prescribed baby food, and our son was happy and healthy again. God was faithful in answering our cries for help, even as He was faithful in fulfilling His promise of a Savior when He sent His Son, Jesus, to this earth.

Yes, I have felt God's comfort when life catches me off-guard. I rejoice in His presence and in the faithful love He shows to me. I know He will be there through the big and little surprises in life. It is that assurance and that comfort I now share with my daughter as I hold her close to my heart.

Prayer: Jesus, You have promised to be with us always. You have promised to send us Your Comforter. You have promised Your presence in our time of need. You have promised Your love and forgiveness at all times. Thank You for keeping Your promises. Amen.

Reflection: How has the Lord comforted you in your time of sorrow?

Let the name of the LORD be praised, both now and forevermore.
From the rising of the sun to the place where it sets the name of the LORD
is to be praised." (Psalm 113:2–3)

SINGING GOD'S PRAISES

My time on the porch has been unsatisfying. I've spent the last few minutes reading my Bible, and now I sit with it open next to me. Today, I've found no glimmer of insight, no feeling of wonder, no flash of understanding. I have felt far from God lately, and reading His Word has been very matter-of-fact.

It's been that way for quite a few days now, and I long for the Lord's presence deep inside my heart. Although I know my life with God is based on His grace and not my feelings, I can't help but yearn for more.

It seems as though I'm in a spiritual desert. Over and over during this time, I've had to remind myself that true faith is the Holy Spirit's work in me, not an emotion. Over and over I've had to tell myself that God is at work in my life even if my mind can't grasp this. But I haven't been listening very well.

Then, somewhere off in the side yard, I hear singing. It's Emily. My daughter likes to make up songs as she walks along. She's too far away for me to make out the words, but I strain to hear anyway.

The same breeze that carries the soft scent of lilacs across the yard now carries Emily's voice too. "Oh, God, You are so great!" she sings. "You are good, and You are kind, and I love You! You are a great God! Great! Great! Great!"

I smile at Emily's enthusiastic faith. As I listen to my daughter, I can't help but be reminded of the Scripture passage: "Let everything that has breath praise the LORD!" (Psalm 150:6). So I open my mouth and start singing quietly. "Oh, God, You are so great! You are good, and You are kind, and I love You! You are a great God! Great! Great! Great!"

When I'm finished, I sing Emily's song again. And again. And again. Over and over I sing it—getting a little louder each time—until I feel the words are coming from my heart. My joy bubbles over as I recall all the wondrous things God has done for me.

It's time to add my own words—to express to the Lord my joy at being His beloved child. "God, You are my Rock, my Comfort, and my Peace. You are the one who makes my life complete. You are my all and all. You are everything I need. You are my Lord and Savior. Today and always, I love to sing Your praises!" The words flow effortlessly, as if it is impossible not to praise the Lord.

As the last note of my song disappears into the air, I feel a peace settle over me. I no longer feel far away from God. The Lord has drawn me closer to Himself.

Prayer: Heavenly Father, today I want to celebrate the wonder of who You are and what You have done in my life—from the gift of Your Son to be my Savior to the gift of faith to the many blessings I enjoy. I want to sing Your praises for all the world to hear! In Jesus' name. Amen.

Reflection: What will you include in your song to God?

*"Everyone who drinks this water will be thirsty again,
but whoever drinks the water I give him will never thirst.
Indeed, the water I give him will become in him a spring of water
welling up to eternal life." (John 4:13–14)*

LIVING WATER

The tangled masses of petunias in the flower boxes that hang from the porch rails have a decided droop this hot summer afternoon. Instead of running for the watering can, I pause to remember the joy these flowers' brilliant colors have brought to my summer. Seeing their flamboyant pinks, radiant reds, and royal purples has never failed to brighten my day. I marvel at how the small plants I started with in May have grown into a jungle of vines, leaves, and petals that cascade over the sides of the boxes in a futile effort to escape. Mostly, though, I think how the abundant masses of flowers that are now turning spindly and brown are a lot like how I'm feeling inside.

There's a dryness to my life—a distance from God. I know that's because the busyness of summer has crowded God and time with Him out of my daily routine. Instead of letting God's Word be "a lamp to my feet and a light for my path" (Psalm 119:105), my Bible sits unopened and unread on the desk in my office. Likewise, my prayers have turned into arrows shot up to heaven without any thought. I've let myself become too busy to spend time with my Best Friend.

I know the Holy Spirit is calling me to do spiritually for myself what I need to do physically for my flowers. We both need water—plain old H_2O for the plants but Living Water for me. It's time to be reconnected to the Source—to become immersed in living streams that will quench the dryness in my life.

I turn back to the house to gather two essentials: my Bible and the watering can. From there I'll head to my swing and turn this dry summer day into a shower full of blessings as I spend time with God in His Word.

Prayer: Father, in Your Son, You have supplied my life with the Living Water. Always keep me thirsting after You. In times of dryness, pour Your Spirit on my thirsty life and refresh me with Your presence as I spend time with You in Your Word and gather with my fellow believers at Your Table. In Jesus' name. Amen.

Reflection: How is God active in Your life to relieve areas of spiritual dryness?

We love because He first loved us. (1 John 4:19)

BOUQUET OF LOVE

Emily and I are spending a few minutes on the porch steps, enjoying cold, fruity Popsicles on this hot summer day. As Emily's treat begins to melt, she begins to walk—thinking, my guess is, that she can escape the dripping stickiness.

I'm not concerned about my daughter wandering too far. On the sidewalk I spy a Popsicle-stained trail of red dots that marks her way. It's a bit like the bread-crumb trail Hansel and Gretel left behind to find their way home through the woods. By connecting the dots, Emily and I can easily find each other again.

I close my eyes for a few moments and feel the sun's hot rays soak into my skin. Around the corner of the house, I hear Emily carrying on a conversation with an imaginary friend. *What is she up to?* I ask myself. It isn't long before I have my answer. Emily heads toward me with a small bouquet of flowers clutched in her hand.

"These flowers are for you," she announces, thrusting the blooms my way.

Her fingers are still so sticky from the Popsicle that I know I will I have to peel the stems from her hand. "They're lovely," I say at the same time I notice that my daughter has raided my flower beds to present me with this bouquet. Yes, these are the colorful zinnias, tall black-eyed susans, yellow sundrops, and delicate pink coreopsis that I planted at the beginning of the season.

"Can we put these in water?" Emily asks.

"Sure," I say with a smile. "Let's go inside and find a vase."

As I get up from my seat, I am stopped by the sight of Emily standing there with her bouquet held tightly in her hand. Reflected in her, I see a picture of myself holding up an offering to my heavenly Father.

All I have to give my Lord—my love, my life, my work—are offered in response to His great love for me. Scripture says: "We love because He first loved us" (1 John 4:19). His love has been shown to me in innumerable ways, but never more dramatically than in the gift of His Son to be my Savior.

Emily's gift has helped me understand what John wrote a little better. Her gift of flowers that I planted has helped me understand there is nothing I can give to God that He—in His generosity—hasn't already given to me.

As I take the blossoms from Emily's hand, I know my daughter has involved me in a valuable lesson today. I also know she is offering me more than flowers. What she extends is a bouquet of love.

Prayer: Jesus, because of Your love for me, You extended Your hands and yielded to the cross. Thank You for Your sacrifice and through it Your gift of forgiveness and eternal life. Amen.

Reflection: What bouquet of love will you offer to the Lord today?

Therefore, if anyone is in Christ, he is a new creation; the old has gone, the new has come! (2 Corinthians 5:17)

SUMMER RAIN

After a day that feels almost too hot to bear, a gentle rain begins to fall. Its steady drops wash the heat out of the air and clean off the thin layer of dust that has settled on the trees and flowers. I sit on the swing, listening to the drumming on the roof and watching the circles that form in the lake as the rain falls. The ducks are swimming around, *quacking* their enjoyment at this midday shower. Soon the geese add their deeper honks of delight. It's like a summertime concert all around me.

In only a short time, the rain stops. The sun comes out from behind the gray clouds and pierces the water droplets that hang on the flowers in the boxes. The drops shine like diamonds. There's a new feel to the day. A freshness. A sense of starting over. I feel like I've been given a clean slate.

Days like this make me thankful I'm a Christian. They remind me in a vivid way that through my Baptism, I became a new creation. They remind me, too, that in our continuing relationship, God offers to me forgiveness for Jesus' sake on a moment by moment basis. The Bible says: "If we confess our sins, He is faithful and just and will forgive us our sins and purify us from all unrighteousness" (1 John 1:9). I have only to ask His pardon and my sins are remembered no more. I love the promise I find in Scripture: "For as high as the heavens are above the earth, so great is His love for those who fear Him; as far as the east is from the west, so far has He removed our transgressions from us" (Psalm 103:11–12).

The fact is that God has brought me into His family. Through the waters of Baptism, He has made me His own. He claims me as His child and has given me the gift of the Holy Spirit, who connects me to Christ. That wonderful gift never fails to give me pause. I've done nothing to deserve this—and I never can do anything to earn or keep it. All of this—life and salvation—comes from God's grace, His undeserved love. My new creation is God's gift freely given—just as He gave Jesus to build a bridge between Himself and humanity so we might know the forgiveness and life that Jesus won for us through His death and resurrection. Forgiveness that washes us clean and removes our sins. Forgiveness—like a gentle, summer rain.

Prayer: Abba, Father, Your love for me is amazing and, at times, overwhelming. Thank You that, because of Jesus, I can come before You to confess my sins and walk away a new creation. In His name I pray. Amen.

Reflection: What brings you before God's throne of forgiveness today?

"For where your treasure is, there your heart will be also." (Matthew 6:21)

FEATHER HUNT

There's a treasure hunt going on in my front yard today. It's the time of year when our geese are molting, and all around the yard beautiful black, gray, and white feathers lie on the ground. A friend of Tim's has said he'll pay 10 cents a feather, and he wants all the boys can collect. He'll use them in his business as a custom sign painter.

Suddenly it's as though we have gold lying in the grass around our house. For days the boys have been running around the yard, picking up feathers. Once their hands are full, they drop their riches into a bag, then they run off to search some more. I've even seen them chasing the geese across the yard in an attempt to loosen a few more feathers.

I can imagine the visions of comic books, candy, and gum that must be dancing through my sons' heads. Each feather they gather represents another coin in their piggy banks. Each feather they find brings them a little closer to the latest toy that they believe will make their lives perfect—at least until a newer and better version comes along.

Part of me wants to leave my seat on the porch and join my boys in this mad dash for riches. That's because part of me is all too familiar with the lure of the treasure the world has to offer. Often I get caught in the mind-set that what the world gives will provide the satisfaction and fulfillment I want in life. At times I have believed that I need more "things" to show my worth as a person—yet I know deep in my heart that is the opposite of what the Lord says.

God's Word tells me: "Do not store up for yourselves treasures on earth, where moth and rust destroy, and where thieves break in and steal. But store up for yourselves treasures in heaven, where moth and rust do not destroy, and where thieves do not break in and steal" (Matthew 6:19–20.) Throughout the Scriptures, Jesus told His followers to leave behind what was important to them—whether it was their nets, their families, or their homes—and follow Him. He demonstrated for them repeatedly that earthly gain wasn't important—faith in Him and the riches of heaven were of eternal significance.

Sometimes I'm so busy chasing after my earthly rewards that I forget the real treasure in my life is Jesus, the forgiveness He earned for me on the cross, and His promise of eternal life with Him. Tonight I'll take some time to remind myself—and my boys—of that fact. I'll gather my Bible and my sons around me, and I'll point them toward the treasure that is richer than all others—the treasure that is Jesus.

Prayer: Jesus, You are worthy above all else to receive glory and honor and praise. You are a treasure beyond compare, and You have given me true riches. Send the Holy Spirit to keep me focused on You. Amen.

Reflection: Is there a "treasure" in your life that has taken precedence over Your faith in God?

Two are better than one. (Ecclesiastes 4:9)

FRIENDS

This afternoon our yard is full of activity. It seems every child in the neighborhood has decided that this is the place to play.

There are several boys in the side yard with Micah, trying out the dirt bike ramps they worked so hard to build over the past few days. Out by the lake, our neighbors Aaron and Josiah are circling the water on their own private expedition for fish and frogs. In the driveway, Steven and his buddy, Jack, have a wild street hockey game going, while Emily is busy playing by the porch steps with her friend, Sarah.

I'm glad our yard is such a busy place. I've always prayed that the lives of my children would be enriched by good friends. Today demonstrates that my prayer has been answered. "Thank You, Lord," I whisper.

Even as I speak those words, I think about all the people who have graced my life with their friendship. I can still feel the chill of the December night when I shared this porch swing with Jayne and confided to her my dreams for the year to come. I can taste the sweetness of the iced tea that Linda and I drank that summer afternoon we rocked and talked for hours on end. And I can still hear the pop of fireworks exploding in the front yard as Barb and I leaned against the porch rail in companionable silence, watching our children enjoy the brilliant bursts of color and light.

I've shared this porch with many different friends, and each time I do, I feel wrapped in the warmth and acceptance that true friendship brings. Jayne, Linda, and Barb are the kind of friends who would do anything for me—watch my children, pitch in with a project, listen to my problems, celebrate my triumphs, dry my tears. Through them, I've come to understand the Scripture passage that says: "A friend loves at all times" (Proverbs 17:17).

I have another friend who shares this porch with me even more regularly. That friend is Jesus, and He has been here to share every moment of my life. Yet Jesus is more than my friend. He is my Savior, my Redeemer, and the Lord of my life. John 15:13 tells me: "Greater love has no one than this, that one lay down his life for his friends." Jesus reached out to me with that "greater love" when He died on the cross for my sins.

Today, as I sit on my porch, surrounded by a yard full of friendship, I am grateful for my greatest friend—Jesus.

Prayer: Heavenly Father, I thank You for the abundance of friends You have placed in my life. Even more, I thank You for my best friend and Savior, Jesus. In His name I pray. Amen.

Reflection: How will you tell your friends how much they mean to you?

Cast all your anxieties on Him.
(1 Peter 5:7)

WHO'S IN CONTROL?

From my front porch perch, I watch Micah and Steven fish. Their fishing styles are as different as their personalities. Micah baits his hook, casts his line, and sits patiently, waiting for a bite. Steven baits his hook, casts his line, and waits patiently—for about 10 seconds. Then he reels his line back in to make sure the worm hasn't been eaten away, casts back out, reels his line back in because he thought he saw the bobber moving, casts back out, reels his line back in to put a bigger worm on the hook, casts back out ...

As I watch my youngest son, I smile at his antics. This isn't the quiet, relaxing recreation I've always known fishing to be. Instead, Steven makes it look like a high-energy sport. I feel tired just watching him.

Steven's impatience while waiting for the perfect catch reminds me of my own impatience while waiting for the answer to my prayers. So many times as I sit here on the swing, I cast my prayers out, believing that "in all things God works for the good of those who love Him, who have been called according to His purpose" (Romans 8:28). Yet many times, only a few minutes pass before I find myself mentally reeling those same prayers back in because it feels like these are things I could take care of without God's help.

Cast them out; reel them in. Cast them out; reel them in. My prayer strategy is as exhausting as Steven's fishing strategy.

As I continue to watch Steven's busyness, my smile fades and a sadness creeps over me. What Steven is doing isn't really causing any harm. Granted, he may be losing fish, but he's really not hurting anything. The same cannot be said for me.

My "fishing" style of prayer tells my heavenly Father, "God, I don't trust that You know what's best for me in this situation or that You understand how I'm feeling right now. So I'll just handle this myself." When I pray like that, it's like telling the Lord that He isn't trustworthy. That He isn't reliable. That He doesn't care.

Not only do I know in my heart that's not true, I know from God's Word that it isn't true. The apostle Peter writes: "Cast all your anxiety on Him because He cares for you" (1 Peter 5:7). There's no stipulation at the end of that sentence. No statement of condition. God doesn't care for me sometimes. He doesn't care for me if I'm living my life perfectly (as if I could). The Bible tells me that God cares for me. Period. And the God who cares for me cares enough to answer my prayers in the way that's best for me.

Steven's activity out on the dock continues, and again I smile, though more knowingly this time. As I bring my cares and concerns to the Lord, I cast them out with a new perspective. "They're all Yours, Lord," I whisper as I imagine myself cutting the line to which my prayers are tied. "They're all Yours."

Prayer: Father, You are trustworthy and reliable, and I know You desire the best for me. Forgive me for Jesus' sake for the times I want to take control of things. Help me to loosen my grip on my life and to place myself in Your merciful hands. In Jesus' name. Amen.

Reflection: What particular areas of your life do you cast to the Lord, then try to reel back in? Ask Him to increase your trust in Him.

But Jesus told him, "Follow Me."
(Matthew 8:22)

Follow the Leader

I've observed several games of Follow the Leader as I've sat on the porch this summer.

Throughout these warmer months, I've noticed how the brown ducks and mallards always hang back and wait for the white ducks to do things first. When I show up on the porch to throw out stale bread or crackers, it's the white ducks that come running first. The brown ducks fall in line behind them.

Then there was the day I received a phone call from my neighbor Paula, who lives on the busy main street behind our home. "You won't believe this," she told me, "but your geese just stopped traffic in front of my house."

It seems the geese had decided to leave the lake located on the other side of the street to come to our lake. Because the two adult geese were losing feathers, they couldn't fly the short distance. Instead, they led their goslings, single file, across four busy lanes of traffic. Their procession brought cars and trucks to a halt.

By the time I got out to the front porch, the geese had made their way through several backyards and were gliding behind one another on the lake. *Your goslings must really trust you,* I thought. *They must know you won't lead them into danger.*

That same wholehearted trust and follow-the-leader attitude is the way I want my faith life to be. I want to follow God with unswerving devotion. Where He leads, I want to follow. Yet there are times I pull back. *This looks a little scary, Lord,* I think. *Are You sure this is the way I'm supposed to go?* Only by the power of the Holy Spirit do my steps continue moving forward in the paths God has chosen for me. Only by the power of the Holy Spirit do I trust that God knows what is best for my life.

I am delighted to be a follower of Christ, and I proudly wear the name of Christian. Jesus tells me, "I am the light of the world. Whoever follows Me will never walk in darkness, but will have the light of life" (John 8:12). Day by day, the Holy Spirit helps me to follow my Leader, and together we walk in the light.

Prayer: Jesus, You are an everlasting light for my path. Forgive me for the times I stray from You. Send the Holy Spirit to help me follow You all of my days. Amen.

Reflection: How does the Holy Spirit help you follow more closely in the steps of your leader, Jesus?

The LORD does not look at the things man looks at.
Man looks at the outward appearance, but God looks at the heart.
(1 Samuel 16:7)

LESSON FROM A BUTTERFLY

As I sit on the porch swing in the late afternoon sun, I see a small butterfly on the rail in front of me. My eyes quickly go past it, barely noticing that its light gray wings are folded up tightly. Only seconds later, as my gaze again turns that way, I watch in astonishment as the butterfly slowly spreads its wings to reveal an amazing array of colors on the inside. Sparkling royal blues, deeper indigos, and flecks of gold decorate the inside of the gossamer wings. I am surprised by the beauty I did not expect.

God often surprises me with beauty. Not only does He do it through the vast array of His creation—from colorful bugs to brilliant summer flowers to breath-taking sunsets—but He does it through people. He does it through the kindness they show, the way they live their lives, the beauty they have inside even though the outside may not be spectacular. When I least expect it, God brings someone my way to remind me to see the world through His eyes.

The reason the Lord does this—and He does it over and over again—is because I am too quick to judge others.

Although I am well-acquainted with Jesus' command to "stop judging by mere appearances" (John 7:24), I struggle with that more often than I care to admit. Someone's slight frown, dirty clothes, or unkempt appearance can cause me to form a quick, negative opinion. Yet when my thoughts start going in that direction, I know I've lost God's perspective. I've lost sight of the fact that being attractive or physically fit or financially secure isn't what matters—at least not to God. What matters to my heavenly Father, and what should matter to me, is the condition of a person's heart.

God continues to invite me to take more time to get to know people for who they are instead of stopping at what they look like. Before I rush to judgment, I can let others spread their wings and show me the brilliant beauty they have inside.

Prayer: Heavenly Father, forgive me for Jesus' sake for the times I make snap judgments. Help me to see past outward appearances and into people's hearts—and help others to do the same for me. Through Your Holy Spirit, make me beautiful on the inside. Make my heart pure, God, so all I do may be pleasing to You. In Jesus' name. Amen.

Reflection: How does God help you to pay more attention to the inward appearance of others?

For we are to God the aroma of Christ.
(2 Corinthians 2:15)

SWEET FRAGRANCE

From across the yard, the smoky smell of food cooking on a backyard grill drifts onto the porch. I lift my head and inhale the tantalizing aroma. I've had my dinner, but my stomach growls in protest at not sharing such a delicious-smelling meal. Wouldn't the chef be surprised if I just knocked on the door and invited myself to dinner?

"What smells so good?" Micah asks from the front yard.

"Someone's making dinner on a charcoal grill," I tell him.

Micah closes his eyes and inhales deeply in response. "Ahhhh!" he sighs as he exhales. "I wish I could have dinner at that house."

As I continue enjoying the savory smells that drift from my neighbor's yard, I'm reminded that the Bible tells me that as a Christian my life is an aroma of God's love to others. Paul writes: "Thanks be to God, who always leads us in triumphal procession in Christ and through us spreads everywhere the fragrance of the knowledge of Him" (2 Corinthians 2:14).

Lord, how can I spread "the aroma of Christ" to my neighbors? I silently ask. In response, I consider two of

God's commands: "Be kind and compassionate to one another" (Ephesians 4:32) and "Therefore, as we have opportunity, let us do good to all people" (Galatians 6:10).

I realize there are a multitude of ways I can spread the aroma of Christ while working for good in the lives of my neighbors. I can stop for a few minutes to chat over the fence with a neighbor as I walk up the driveway to the mailbox. I can share a plate of cookies or homemade bread. I can help an elderly neighbor with a job that's easy for me but difficult for him. I can say a prayer for each one—for health, for happiness, for the gift of faith in Jesus as Savior.

The Lord presents to me many opportunities to spread the sweet perfume of the Gospel to all those around me. Through the power of His Holy Spirit in my life, I am able to do all these things. In my neighborhood, the Holy Spirit is helping me to be the aroma of Christ.

Prayer: Heavenly Father, I am blessed to know that because of Christ's sacrifice for me, my life is a sweet, fragrant offering to You. In His name I pray. Amen.

Reflection: How is God working in your life right now and how will you share that sweet perfume with others?

Do not let the sun go down while you are still angry. (Ephesians 4:26)

RECONCILIATION

The heat of the summer evening is nothing compared to the heat of the anger I have boiling inside of me. Tim and I both had frustrating days. I spent mine dealing with three children who couldn't get along. Tim spent his dealing with "unreasonable, demanding clients" as he put it. Right after dinner, our tempers reached the boiling point, and we took our frustrations out on each other.

First, someone—and I honestly don't remember who it was—snapped out an answer to a simple question. Then someone else's tone of voice showed anger at the person being addressed. Before we knew it, we were fighting over things that had nothing to do with the events of the day. Bottled up frustrations came spilling out as the two of us fought to be right. Soon the room overflowed with angry words and feelings. Finally, I walked out the front door—shutting it loudly behind me to make my point.

Out here on the porch, I expect my anger to lessen, but it doesn't. *God,* I rant, *how can Tim be so infuriating? Can't he see he's wrong?!*

I came outside so I wouldn't say something to Tim that I would later regret. I expect a pat on the back for my strategic retreat. None comes.

Sitting here in the silence, I continue to voice my frustrations to the Lord—secretly hoping He'll take my side. Of course, I know that won't happen. Instead a breeze kicks up, and slowly—very slowly—my anger begins to cool.

I know God doesn't take sides in a disagreement where both people speak angry words. I also know from my experience tonight and from God's Word that "a gentle answer turns away wrath, but a harsh word stirs up anger" (Proverbs 15:1). Neither Tim nor I had a gentle answer for the other on this day, and I can see the mess it's made for the two of us.

Now that the heat of the moment has passed, I ask the Lord to forgive me for my harsh words. I ask Him to show me Tim's perspective on what happened this evening. A Bible passage comes to mind: "Everyone should be quick to listen, slow to speak and slow to become angry, for man's anger does not bring about the righteous life that God desires" (James 1:19–20).

I ask God to help me live the righteous life He desires and help me change my behavior to follow Christ's example of love. I know my words and actions weren't the way I should treat my husband—or anyone else. I know it's time to apologize to Tim as well. I get up from the swing just as the front door opens and Tim emerges. "Are we done fighting?" he asks.

"I think so, but I still have something to say to you," I tell him as I cross the porch.

"I have something to say to you too," he replies.

There on the porch, with the sun slowing sinking on the horizon, we put our arms around each other and ask for each other's forgiveness. In the warmth of the setting sun, I bask in my husband's love and forgiveness and in the assurance of my Father's love and forgiveness as well. Our anger is forgotten.

Prayer: Heavenly Father, help me to control my temper and to keep open the lines of communication in my marriage. In Jesus' name. Amen.

Reflection: How does the Lord help you to control your temper?

Let him who boasts boast in the Lord.
For it is not the one who commends himself
who is approved, but the one whom the Lord commends.
(2 Corinthians 10:17–18)

BRAGGING RIGHTS

This evening a competition unfolds before me on the basketball court in our driveway. "Micah," Steven taunts, "I can make this shot, and you can't." Although my younger son is a head shorter than his brother, Steven puts forth his challenge with all the bravado of a seven-foot-tall professional basketball player.

"No, you can't," Micah replies. Like most older brothers, he hates any threat to his authority and ability.

"Then play me," Steven's challenge continues.

"You're on," Micah agrees, and the game begins.

Throughout the contest, Steven's boasts continue until his words start to grow mean-spirited. "Take some lessons. You're pitiful!" he says as he muscles forward to grab a rebound. "What a wimp!"

As the minutes click by, Steven's lead lengthens considerably. His last shot goes through the hoop with a satisfying swish. "I win!" Steven shouts, punctuating his triumph with a victory dance. Micah throws the ball at his brother and walks into the house.

"Hey, Mom," Steven calls, "did you see that? I beat Micah!"

"I saw," I call back. "And I heard. What happened to good sportsmanship out there?"

"I can't help that I'm better than him!" Steven replies, not ready to admit his guilt and even more reluctant to give up his bragging rights.

"But you can help your attitude and your words," I remind him. "I heard a lot of bragging and put-downs out there. Is that any way to treat your brother?"

"I guess not," Steven reluctantly agrees.

"So what now?" I ask him.

"An apology?" Steven answers.

"An apology," I agree.

As Steven leaves to look for Micah, I feel a stirring in my heart. That's usually a signal that I've spoken a truth I haven't put into practice in my own life. *Lord, I'm not like that, am I?* I ask. *Arrogant? Boastful?* In reply, Jesus' words come to mind: "If anyone wants to be first, he must be the very last, and the servant of all" (Mark 9:35).

Unlike Steven, it's usually not boastful words or an in-your-face victory dance that gets me into trouble. It's usually the attitude of my heart. While there may be a smile on my face, there are times when my spirit is filled with grumbling and griping because I'm not appreciated, recognized, or applauded for all I do. Although those around me may not see my unservant-like attitude, my heavenly Father does. It amazes me to think that He sees everything I do and still loves me. But He does love me—loves me enough to give His Son to be my Savior. Loves me enough to work through His Spirit to make me a new creation. Loves me enough to enable me to do His will.

As for me, I love God enough to want those things too. I want to live a life worthy of my Lord. I want to make my Father proud.

Prayer: Heavenly Father, forgive me for Jesus' sake for the times my words and actions don't reflect the joy I have as Your child. Bless the words of my mouth so my boasting may be of Your work in my life. In Jesus' name. Amen.

Reflection: What recent victory has God given you so you can boast of Him?

There is a time for everything, and a season for every activity under heaven.
(Ecclesiastes 3:1)

HINT OF AUTUMN

As I make my way to the porch, I notice a new coolness to the evening. Although the calendar still tells me it's summer, I feel a dampness in the air and smell a mustiness in the breeze. Even the summer wind whispers of changes to come: Gone are the slow, laid-back days of summer. Here comes the more hectic pace of fall.

I sigh as I wonder if I'm ready for this transition. I like the comfort of the old and familiar. I like to take new experiences and challenges slowly. Sometimes, I admit, I'd rather not deal with change at all.

Lately, though, I've noticed quite a few changes—mostly in my children. Micah, Steven, and I spent several days over the last few weeks doing all the inevitable back-to-school shopping. Not only were there new backpacks and school supplies to buy, but new clothes and shoes too. It's hard to believe I'm once again shopping for bigger sizes and that the boys are advancing another grade at school. As much as I'd like to, I can't deny that my children are growing up—and that it's happening much too quickly.

As I sit here, I admit that there are aspects of my children's newfound independence that I love. Just as I cheered when Micah, Steven, and Emily all took their first steps, I now cheer as they continue to walk in new directions, find their paths in life, and make their own decisions—large and small.

Yet there are also things I dislike—like the inevitable pulling away, especially by my sons, as my children want to do more things on their own. "Thanks, but I can do it myself" is a constant refrain at our house. I try my best to remember that Scripture tells me there will be "a time to be silent and a time to speak" (Ecclesiastes 3:7b), but it's hard not to be needed as much anymore. I know I should give them room, but so often I want to offer my hand.

Just as my heavenly Father allows me the freedom to choose, I can allow my children freedom too. As they grow, my prayer follows each one that they will turn to the Lord with their questions and decisions. I want them to find God's Word to be a lamp to their feet and a light for their path (Psalm 119:105). I want them to know that when they feel burdened they can turn to Jesus and He will give them rest (Matthew 11:28). I want them to know how much God loves and cares for them (John 3:16). Amid all the changes they face now, and the many changes to come, God's forgiving and sustaining love always will be available.

Prayer: Father, though life may be full of changes, Your merciful love and gracious care for me and my family are constant. Thank You for Your faithfulness in our lives. In Jesus' name. Amen.

Reflection: What changes are you facing that you need God's help with right now?

Let everything that has breath praise the LORD. (Psalm 150:6)

SUMMER'S BLESSINGS

This evening I shield my eyes against the rays of sunshine that slant under the eaves of the porch roof and blind me with their brilliance. Even here there is no escaping the relentless intensity or heat of the sun. I shut my eyes to the brightness and lean back into the porch swing, letting its rhythmic rocking soothe my spirit. All around me I hear the sounds of summer: children shouting, lawnmowers whirring, sprinklers running.

All too soon these lazy days will pass, but before they do, I want to spend a few moments thinking back over the blessings these last three sun-drenched months have brought. I remember simple things:

- The luscious taste of the first watermelon of the season and the feel of its juices running down my chin.
- The smell of dinner being grilled outside.
- The colorful masses of petunias, impatiens, marigolds, zinnias, and coreopsis that decorate the porch and yard.
- The impromptu picnics we've shared with family and friends.
- Watching the boys' synchronized movements as they paddle a canoe across the lake.
- The pop of firecrackers as they proclaim the glorious freedom we enjoy.

- The hiss of the garden hose and the shouts of my children as they run through its cooling spray.

- Savoring a tall glass of pink lemonade with a friend.

- The boys' shouts of "I've got a big one!" that interrupt a quiet evening of fishing.

- The prickly feel of newly mown grass under bare feet.

- Emily's delight as she finds another fuzzy dandelion to blow.

- The nighttime serenade of crickets and frogs.

- Lying under the stars to show my children the Big Dipper.

- The glittering beauty of fireflies as they light up their own small piece of the summer darkness.

For me, summer is a time of light—the light of the sunshine that brightens the season, the light that glows from special times spent with family and friends, the light of God's love reflected all around me.

Soon the pace of life will increase. School will begin, and commitments will increase. Until then, I turn my face to the sun to thank and praise my heavenly Father for His summer blessings.

Prayer: Heavenly Father, I praise You for this season of sunshine and fun. Thank You for time outside and for the enjoyment Your creation brings. Thank You for the ability to share Your love and forgiveness with those around me. In Jesus' name. Amen.

Reflection: How have you experienced the light of God's blessings in simple ways this season?

SILHOUETTES

After the coolness of the air-conditioned house, the porch's warmth wraps around me like a blanket as I head to my place on the swing. Tonight Micah has asked a few too many questions for which I don't have satisfactory answers—at least not for him. He asked me about peer pressure, about the pursuit of right and wrong, and why it's so hard at times to make wise decisions. As we talked, the unasked question hung in the air, "Why can't I just choose the easy way instead of God's way?"

I know how my son feels. How many times have I wanted to take the smooth and easy path instead of the more difficult one along which God is guiding me?

Because I didn't have sufficient answers for my son, I retreated to the porch to find some answers from God. Now as I swing, the evening sky continues to darken, and the trees out by the road take on a stark silhouette. There is no gray in the picture I see before me now. It is as simple and as clear as black and white. *Why isn't life more like that, Lord?* I wonder. *Why isn't it more clearly defined?*

Life in Me is, God reminds me through His Word. Jesus

is the Truth (John 14:6). There is black and white. Good and evil. Right and wrong. God hasn't blurred the picture. I have.

I squirm uncomfortably in my seat. To know the truth of God's Word and believe in Him is one thing. To know that His Word and His Holy Spirit permeate my life, my decisions, and my future is another.

Yet I have no choice. Jesus tells me, "I am the Way and the Truth and the Life" (John 14:6). Because Jesus is in my life, because I believe that He is my Lord and Savior, then He will help me to live according to His truth. I can't live according to this truth by my own strength. Jesus walks with me through all the events of my life, guiding me in His truth and leading me in righteousness. I can remind Micah that he, too, has only to ask for the Lord's help when tough decisions come his way. God will be there to walk with and guide him too.

I know each night the trees' stark outline will serve as a visual reminder of the dilemmas and choices I'll face each day. I know, too, that Jesus will help me face each one with confidence. Tomorrow evening I'll bring Micah out here to share with him how God cares for His children and the reality that absolutes do exist.

Prayer: Father, help me to raise my children in the light of Your truth so they may shine that light in a world that often appears too gray. Help me point them to Jesus as the Way, the Truth, and the Life. In His name. Amen.

Reflection: What gray areas of your life do you need to turn over to God?

Then I acknowledged my sin to You and did not cover up my iniquity. I said, "I will confess my transgressions to the LORD"—and You forgave the guilt of my sin. (Psalm 32:5)

SECRETS

The heat of the summer night presses against me as I lazily rock on the porch swing. To my surprise, Micah joins me, settling at the other end of the seat. At first we sit in silence, enjoying the night sounds of frogs croaking and crickets chirping. After a few moments, Micah starts to talk.

First, he tells me about the things he'd still like to do before the summer is over. Then, slowly, he shares his ambitions for the future and some goals he's set for himself. I smile, knowing that in the safety and security of the dark he feels free to open up. I feel that way too. The dark is conducive for telling secrets.

There have been many times I've sat here in the dark, sharing my own secrets with God. Here on the porch, with no one around and the blackness surrounding me, I'm able to pour out my heart—the good and the bad—to the Lord. Even as I confess, I realize that God knows my words before I even speak them—for there is no thought that can be withheld from Him (Job 42:2 KJV). There are no secrets from God. Nothing can be hidden from Him.

It's not that God doesn't know my sins. It's that He wants me to confess them. This confessing of my transgressions, this telling of my faults, allows His forgiveness to wash over me. I bring the burden of my sins to my Savior and He "[purifies me] from all unrighteousness" (1 John 2:9). I believe God's promise that "everyone who believes in [Jesus] receives forgiveness of sins through His name" (Acts 10:43).

Confession isn't a process I take lightly. I know it is the very blood of Jesus, shed for me, that cleanses me from my sin (1 John 1:7). That thought never fails to humble me as I realize the height of God's love and the depth of His sacrifice. It's a love He never keeps secret.

Prayer: Heavenly Father, I'm thankful there are no secrets from You and that Your forgiveness is always available when we turn to You in repentance and in Jesus' name. Amen.

Reflections: What secrets will you share with God today?

Where is God my Maker, who gives songs in the night?
(Job 35:10)

SUMMER SYMPHONY

My children stay up later in the summertime. Tonight, as darkness falls, the three of them race inside and beg for a jar to hold the lightning bugs they plan to catch. "The front yard is full of them!" Steven exclaims. I hand him a jar and follow behind to watch this summertime ritual.

Walking outside, I'm amazed at the lights that star the grass and float through the sky. While the boys have immediate success, Emily only manages to catch the warm summer breeze. Time after time when she opens her cupped hands, they are empty. Surprisingly, she doesn't seem to mind.

The gray of night turns to black before the jar is filled with enough light to satisfy my children. The sky has wrapped its dark blue blanket tightly under its chin, reminding me it's time to wrap my children in their own blankets for the night. "Can't we stay up just a little longer?" they beg as I *shoo* them upstairs.

While preparations for bed go on inside, I sit on the steps to enjoy a few minutes of silence. As I sit, I realize the night is anything but quiet. The frogs around the lake already have begun their deep, low night songs while the crickets and locusts have joined in with *chirps* and *whirrs.* There's even an owl somewhere in the dark, hooting its greeting for everyone to hear. Underneath it all is the sound of the wind. The night plays its summertime symphony.

The front door opens, and Micah, Steven, and Emily emerge. They join me on the steps, hoping for a reprieve from bedtime. Before anyone can speak, I put my fingers to my lips. "Listen," I whisper.

I watch as their faces slowly register delight at the noises that surround them. "It sounds like music," Micah whispers back. The other two nod.

"It's one of God's night songs," I tell them. "The Bible says, 'Let everything that has breath praise the LORD' (Psalm 150:6). It sure sounds like nature is praising the Lord tonight, doesn't it?"

The three of them nod and continue to listen. All of us are enthralled at the beauty of this performance. At this moment I can't imagine that even an angelic chorus is any more beautiful than what I am hearing right now. In the dark of the night, my heart sings with joy as I sit surrounded by songs of praise.

Prayer: Heavenly Father, I gladly add my voice to the chorus of those who sing Your praises from sunrise to sunset (Psalm 113:3). In Jesus' name. Amen.

Reflection: When was the last time you listened for one of God's night songs?

When I consider Your heavens, the work of Your fingers, the moon and the stars, which You have set in place, what is man that You are mindful of him, the son of man that You care for him? (Psalm 8:3–4)

How Big Is God?

In the dark quiet of the night, Tim and I sit on the porch steps, gazing up at the stars. We've already found the Big Dipper, the Little Dipper, and Orion's Belt; now we're marveling at all the tiny lights that dot the sky. The longer we look, the more stars there seem to be.

"Makes you feel small, doesn't it?" I ask.

"No, it makes God feel really big," Tim replies.

My husband's answer catches me by surprise. Once again I'm reminded of my tendency to look at life from a less-than-positive perspective. While Tim always has seen that glass of water as half full, to me it's half empty.

I've asked the Lord to help me work on this part of my personality—mostly because I've found it colors more parts of my life than I like. Because of my pessimistic nature, I've found that, at times, I view even my faith life from a negative perspective. When I'm caught up in my troubles, my temptations, and my sins, I forget that "in all these things we are more than conquerors through Him who loved us" (Romans 8:37). I forget that victory doesn't come because of something I do, it comes because God sent Jesus to do all the things I can't—fulfill God's commands, take my punishment on the cross, and rise from the dead. In short, I forget how big God is.

The prophet Isaiah asks: "Who has measured the waters in the hollow of His hand, or with the breadth of His hand marked off the heavens? Who has held the dust of the earth in a basket, or weighed the mountains on the scales and the hills in a balance?" (Isaiah 40:12). The only answer is my God—who is bigger than my problems, bigger than my doubts, bigger than my sin, bigger than death, bigger than any obstacle that interferes with my life as His dear child.

So on nights like this, when I'm reminded just how big God is, I ask the Holy Spirit to help me celebrate the many ways God is active in my life. I want to trust my heavenly Father for all things. I want to look at that glass of water and see it as full to overflowing—just as tonight's sky is full with stars.

Prayer: Heavenly Father, open my eyes to see all You have given to me. Open my arms so they are big enough to embrace the opportunities You bring into my life. Open my heart to the depths of Your love. In Jesus' name. Amen.

Reflection: What negative thoughts limit your ability to appreciate God's actions in your life?

The Season of Abundance

May the LORD bless His land ...
with the best gifts of the earth and its fullness.
(Deuteronomy 33:13, 16)

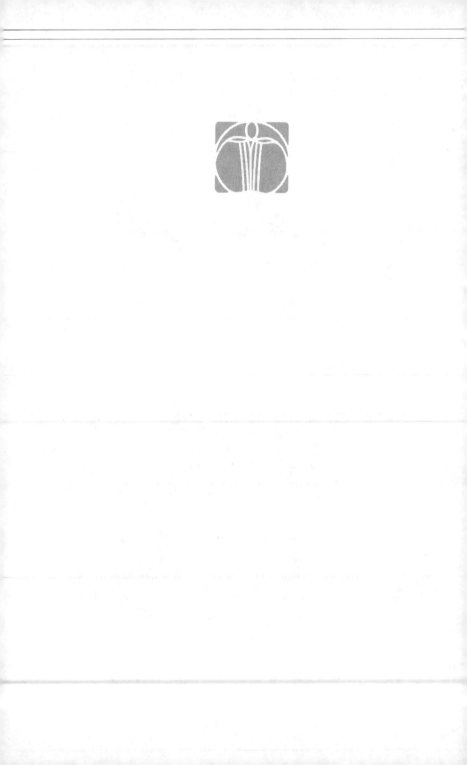

Trust in the LORD with all your heart. (Proverbs 3:5)

LETTING GO

Today is the first day of school. It's that time of year that some of us love and some of us hate. I feel a little bit of both emotions—especially this year.

Part of me wants to jump up and down with joy that the past month of constant bickering and complaints of "There's nothing to do!" is finally over. Another part wants to hold captive the two boys walking down the driveway to the bus stop. I am a mother torn between two choices.

So what do I do? Neither.

Instead, Emily and I stand on the porch, waving to the boys and calling "I love you!" for the whole neighborhood to hear. Steven, still young enough not to be embarrassed, waves and calls back, "I love you too!" Micah, old enough now to be aware of what's cool—and this is not cool—just keeps walking. Not a wave. Not a word.

I brush away the tears that suddenly sting my eyes and swallow again and again in an attempt to get rid of the lump that's formed in my throat. The worst part, though, is the hand that seems to have gripped my heart, squeezing it tighter and tighter and making it difficult to breathe.

Why is letting go so hard? I wonder as I pull Emily close.

My heavenly Father knows about letting go. He knows all about allowing a Son to leave the safe haven of home. "For God so loved the world that He gave His only begotten Son" (John 3:16). When He sent Jesus into this world, God knew the problems Jesus would face—including the painful road to the cross and its torturous death, but God also knew that Jesus' earthly life and death were necessary to restore His fallen children to His kingdom. God knew that it was necessary to send Jesus to His birth in that stable, to His death on that cross, and to His resurrection from that cold tomb.

Today is yet another reminder that God truly understands what is going on in my life. I can trust Him to comfort me as only a parent can when facing the time to let go. I can be assured that because of God's salvation plan, my children and I are protected under the banner of His love, even as they venture to school and, in time, beyond our family home. With such a reassurance, I am ready to encourage my children to test their wings … and fly.

Prayer: Heavenly Father, bless and protect my children while they are gone from me today. Keep them safely in Your care. Strengthen my trust in Your protection and remind me often that You love them even more than I do. In Jesus' name. Amen.

Reflection: What blessings will you ask of God for family members or friends today?

For now we see through a glass, darkly; but then face to face.
(1 Corinthians 13:12 KJV)

EYES OF FAITH

A thick fog has rolled in overnight. This morning as I wander out to the porch, I can't even see the lake. I know the ducks are out there only because I can hear their quacking as they call early morning greetings back and forth. I can't tell, though, where they are on the water—or even if they are on the water at all.

In the gray covering of the fog, I feel isolated. It is as though our entire neighborhood has disappeared. I know there are houses out there, but it truly seems as though it is just God and me out here on the porch this morning. It's a nice feeling.

"Good morning, Lord," I whisper, not wanting to intrude on the silence.

Although this fog brings a sense of intimacy with the Lord, it also brings with it a reminder of what *faith* is. Although I can't see God with my eyes, I believe with every ounce of my being that God exists. There is a knowing, a certainty, deep in my heart that God is real. Because of God's gift of faith, I believe in Him, I believe in the forgiveness that Jesus earned for me on the cross, I believe in the resurrection to come, I trust that God's plans for me are perfect—even though I can't see my heavenly Father.

Of course, there have been times when I have wondered where God was amid everything occurring in my life. Times I have doubted His presence in my life. Times I have even doubted that God cared for me at all. But God sent His Holy Spirit to remind me through Word and Sacrament that God was right there with me. Amidst my trial, God kept His promise to hold my hand and help me. He reminded me that I had nothing to fear (Isaiah 41:13). He was, and is, faithful.

For me, days like today are all about faith—the "substance of things hoped for, the evidence of things not seen" (Hebrews 11:1 KJV). They are about believing that the fog will lift and the sun will shine. They are about trusting that God is active in my life. They are about knowing the day will come when I will see my Lord and Savior face to face. Until then, "My soul waits for the LORD" (Psalm 130:6).

Prayer: Heavenly Father, send Your Holy Spirit to help me wait for You in joyful anticipation. Forgive me for Jesus' sake for the times my impatience causes me to doubt You. Give me eyes of faith to look at the cross and empty tomb and see Your great love for me. Until the day You call me home, help me live according to Your will. In Jesus' name. Amen.

Reflection: How does God help you to see Him with "eyes of faith"?

Ye have need of patience. (Hebrews 10:36 KJV)

PLANTING PROMISES

This morning Emily and I worked in the yard in anticipation of the brilliant colors and sweet smells that will decorate the yard in the spring.

We gathered together the crocus, daffodil, hyacinth, and tulip bulbs that Tim bought earlier in the month, pulled our garden gloves and a trowel from their place on the shelf, and spent the morning "planting promises." With the sun warming our backs and the wind ruffling our hair, I couldn't think of a better way to spend a fall morning.

"Can I dig the first hole?" Emily asked as our task began.

I handed her the trowel and watched her frustrated efforts to make even a small dent in the hard earth. It wasn't long before she looked at me in frustration. "You do it!" she demanded.

"How about if I dig the holes and you drop in the bulbs?" I asked.

Emily nodded. She liked this new arrangement.

As we worked, I showed my helper how to drop each bulb in the hole so its tip faced upward. "That way it can push to the top when the sun warms the ground in the spring," I told Emily.

"I don't want to wait until spring," Emily sulked.

I smiled and told her we had no choice. Seeing her frown, I placed a bulb in her hand. "Remember, we're planting promises. We put the bulbs in *now* to get flowers *later*. We have to wait."

Now as I sit on the porch, I think about this morning and realize how hard it is for my daughter to wait for the work we did today to yield its benefits. Waiting is hard—for my daughter and for me.

Whether it's looking forward to an event in the future, awaiting an answer to prayer, or anticipating the spring flowers that will bloom from newly planted bulbs, I don't have much patience for waiting. Like most people, I desire instant gratification. I need things done now—not later. I like to receive answers to my prayers immediately. In short, I simply don't have time to wait.

Patience is a fruit of the Spirit that the Lord cultivates in my life. He wants me to learn that "the end of a matter is better than its beginning, and patience is better than pride" (Ecclesiastes 7:8). As hard as that is for me, I crave a patient spirit. This afternoon I celebrate the gifts that God has planted in my heart—gifts of faith, forgiveness, love, and care. I look forward to seeing these gifts flower and flourish as the Holy Spirit continues to work in my life.

Prayer: Heavenly Father, when I want to race forward and move ahead of You, help me to slow down and patiently wait on You. In Jesus' name. Amen.

Reflection: In what area of your life are you impatiently waiting for God to work? How will God help you to develop patience?

FINDING MY WAY

The sun is shining brightly this morning, and there is a fool-you-with-the-feel-of-summer warmth to the day. The leaves on the trees are still bright green, and they cling tightly to their branches. The summer's flowers are still blooming, though not with their earlier profusion. Their blossoms are less abundant now and less colorful. It's almost as though their hues have been purposely dimmed so as not to compete with the deeper, earthier purples, reds, yellows, and oranges that come with autumn.

From my porch swing, I spy bees sipping the last nectar from the flowers and watch squirrels scurrying across the yard as they look for nuts to store for the winter. Seemingly out of nowhere, a group of small, white butterflies appears. They flutter around in the flower garden—some landing on plants and bushes, others content to just test their wings against the breeze. I notice one butterfly a little apart from the others and watch as it zigzags through the air. It looks to me as if it has lost its way and is unable to get back to the others.

I've been that butterfly. There have been times when I've lost my way—my sense of direction and purpose in life. There have been times when I've asked, "Do I go forward, Lord? How far forward? Will I know when to stop? Or do I stay here?" Because I think I need to make a decision, I start in the direction I think God wants me to go. I want action—after all, there's nothing proactive about waiting. But I haven't stopped to consider what God wants me to do.

Once again, I've forgotten that how I look at life and how God looks at life are different. The apostle Peter writes: "With the Lord a day is like a thousand years, and a thousand years are like a day" (2 Peter 3:8). While time may feel like it's standing still to me, I can be assured that God is still at work.

Over and over in my life, God has reminded me through His Word that His timing is perfect. He is "the Alpha and the Omega, the First and the Last, the Beginning and the End" (Revelation 22:13). What a privilege to trust the eternal God, who has made me His own through the gift of faith in His precious Son.

Prayer: Heavenly Father, even when I don't know the direction, I trust that You are leading me in the paths I should go. You are always beside me with Your forgiveness, Your love, and Your grace as we travel the road of life together. In Jesus' name. Amen.

Reflection: How is God leading you in your life right now?

And I pray that you, being rooted and established in love, may have power, together with all the saints, to grasp how wide and long and high and deep is the love of Christ, and to know this love that surpasses knowledge —that you may be filled to the measure of all the fullness of God. (Ephesians 3:17–19)

GOD'S LOVE

Sitting here in the quiet of the front porch, my daughter's words echo in my ears. I can still hear the exasperation in her voice. "Mommy," she told me after I had asked her to brush her teeth, make her bed, and take care of her dirty clothes, "I can't do everything at the same time!"

While Emily still needs to tackle one task before moving on to the next, doing "everything at the same time" is second nature to me. I always have two or three activities going on at once. In the morning, I brush my teeth while making the bed. In the afternoon you'll find me making dinner, unpacking backpacks, and returning phone calls. At night, if I do watch TV, you can be sure there's a basket of laundry being folded or sewing on my lap.

I'll admit that I've bought into the performance-based mentality that permeates our culture. Not only can I do it all, I tell myself proudly, but I can do it all *fast*. I've found the more I get done, the better I feel about myself.

Unfortunately, this mind-set has its affects on my spiritual life too. Occasionally I catch myself thinking, *If I can only give more—more money, more time, more talent—then God will love me more.* If I teach Sunday school, run a small group, volunteer for the outreach program—and feel guilty that I'm not doing something else—then I must be where God wants me. Right?

Yet as I sit on the porch swing, Emily's words continue to echo in my ears until they become my prayer: *Lord, I can't do everything. ... As hard as I try, as much as I may want to, I just can't do it.*

Blessedly, God doesn't expect me to be able to do *anything.* Nothing I do can make God love me more. Nothing I do can earn forgiveness or salvation. Everything has already been done for me—by Jesus. God already loves me so much that He sacrificed His Son on the cross to save me from sin, death, and the devil. And because the Holy Spirit has worked faith in Jesus in my heart, I can joyfully respond to all God's unconditional love for me with acts of love and service for others.

Today as I search the Scriptures, I am reminded that God's love "endures forever" (Psalm 136:1) and that my heavenly Father loves me with an "everlasting love" (Jeremiah 31:3). God Himself even tells me, "Though the mountains be shaken and the hills be removed, yet My unfailing love for you will not be shaken" (Isaiah 54:10). Finally, I read again that "God so loved the world that He gave His one and only Son, that whoever believes in Him shall not perish but have eternal life" (John 3:16). Like so many others, at times I have personalized this passage by replacing the words "the world" with my name. It's time to do that again. It's time to reconnect with the depth of God's love for all His children—including me.

Prayer: Heavenly Father, remind me that You don't love me because of what I do, but You love me because of who You are and what Your Son did when He died on the cross for my sins. In Jesus' name I pray. Amen.

Reflection: What are you basing God's love for you on right now?

"Let the little children come to Me."
(Mark 10:14)

THE FAITH OF A CHILD

The boys haven't arrived home from school yet, and Emily and I sit snuggling on the porch. I push my toe against the floor to keep the swing gently swaying while Emily tells me about her day at preschool. She describes the soft, orange clay for molding pumpkins, the leaf-shaped sponges for painting a fall-colored tree, and the nuts for counting all the way to 10. To top it off, none of her friends was absent, and the snack was one of her favorites—chocolate pudding. *What more could there be in life?* the happiness in her voice tells me.

What more, indeed? I think.

It's wonderful to sit back and look at life from the perspective of my youngest child. Like most children, Emily lives in a world where the smallest things bring the greatest joy. Having her favorite friend to play with at school, making it across the monkey bars without letting go, hearing a new story during circle time, receiving a warm hug good-bye from her teacher ... and knowing that in two days she gets to do it all over again. Now that's living!

Jesus tells me that "the kingdom of God belongs to [children] such as these" (Mark 10:14), and I believe that with all my heart. Emily is a member of God's family. Each day I share with Emily that God loves her, that Jesus died for her sins, and that He rose from the dead so she will one day spend eternity with Him. God is an integral part of our family. Emily is reminded of His presence when we say grace before meals, when she sees me reading my Bible during my quiet time and when I read Bible stories to her, when we pray for someone who's hurt, when we attend church and Sunday school, and when she and I kneel by her bed at the end of the day. God has used me to teach my daughter about Himself.

To my delight, Emily knows and trusts God and His merciful love for her. She believes that Jesus is her Savior. She is on her own walk of faith, beginning with the faith of a child.

Prayer: Father, thank You for these children You have entrusted to my care. I am grateful that You have called me and my children to be part of Your family. Help me to teach my children about You and about Jesus, their Savior. In His name I pray. Amen.

Reflection: In what ways will you ask God to make your faith more childlike?

I will praise You, O LORD, with my heart;
I will tell of all Your wonders. I will be glad and rejoice in You;
I will sing praise to Your name, O Most High. (Psalm 9:1–2)

AUTUMN PRAISE

The brilliant colors of fall surround me, and the day has the feel of a party. Throughout the yard, the plants and trees have donned their fall wardrobes. The spirea bushes on the side of the porch have changed from summer green to autumn gold, while the hostas along the drive have traded in their variegated stripes for a new sunshine yellow hue. The two pear trees out front have decided on a rich burgundy covering to replace the green they've worn all summer, and the holly bushes have draped on necklaces of red berries to add to the festive mood of the day.

Even the wind seems to be in a playful mood as it lifts some fallen leaves in a colorful whirlwind. The leaves look like tiny ballerinas as they twirl and dance through the air. Out in the yard, Emily is twirling and dancing too. It's easy to see that the joyous spirit of the day has taken hold of her as well.

All around me, nature has been transformed for the season by the hand of God. Creation seems to be offering its praises to the Lord through the colors of the trees and bushes, the coolness of the breeze, and the crisp, fresh smell in the air. As I sit on the swing, I gladly join in those praises, "O LORD, our Lord, how majestic is Your name in all the earth!" (Psalm 8:1). Today is one of those days when my heart feels like it could burst within me because it can't contain all the joy I have inside. This is a day when I rejoice in God's love and am inspired by His majesty.

Suddenly I want to shout that news from the top of the roof. "God loves me!" I can picture myself yelling from the peak of our gable. "And He loves you too! Isn't that amazing?"

Yes, today is a day for rejoicing in the awesome beauty of God as seen in the world around me. Today is a day to praise the Lord.

Prayer: Heavenly Father, evidence of Your majesty surrounds me today, and I praise You for the beauty of it all. You are truly God of the whole earth, and all the earth rightly gives You praise. In Jesus' name. Amen.

Reflection: How will you praise the Lord today for His beautiful creation?

For we are God's workmanship. (Ephesians 2:10)

THE THREADS OF MY LIFE

It's not often I take my cross-stitching out to the front porch, but today I grab the bag that holds my supplies and head outside to find a comfortable seat in a rocking chair. As I pull out my latest project, I marvel at the beautiful design that's nearing completion. Tiny x's in various shades of green, pink, white, yellow, and brown floss create a picture of a chair on a front porch. "Very fitting," my friends tell me, knowing the amount of time I spend out here.

Today as I begin stitching, I feel the excitement of knowing this project is almost finished. I love making something beautiful, but even more than that, I love the lessons the Lord has taught me as He's shown me the parallels between this work and the work He's doing in my life.

Years ago when I first began cross-stitching, I saw that when I pulled the threads of a design too tight, the fabric puckered. When I ran a dark thread across a bare area, the outline showed through from the other side. Inevitably, these shortcuts marred the beauty of the finished product. I've kept those pieces to remind myself to take my time and to do my best—which is exactly how God works in my life.

Sometimes God uses His Law to show me areas of my life where I've missed a stitch or left some threads unclipped. Then His Holy Spirit works slowly and carefully through Word and Sacrament to repair my mistakes. The tugging and pulling, snipping and cutting may hurt for the moment, but I know they are a sign the Lord is working to mend the fabric of my life. As the Lord weaves those threads into a pleasing pattern, He doesn't take shortcuts. He is careful and patient to see through to completion the work He has begun in me (Philippians 1:6).

So as I sit here on the porch, I resist the urge to hurry through to the end of my project. Although I'm anxious to be finished, I want to recall the many ways God is at work in my life with each stitch I take.

Prayer: Heavenly Father, thank You for making something beautiful from the tangled threads of my life. In Jesus' name. Amen.

Reflection: What work do you see God doing in your life this week?

Look to the LORD and His strength; seek His face always.
(Psalm 105:4)

EYES OPEN, HEAD UP

It's one of those drop-dead gorgeous days of fall. The maple trees in the front yard haven't yet decided if red or yellow is the color for the season, though they seem to have settled on a brilliant mix of the two hues for this day. The air holds the musty scent of chrysanthemums and fallen leaves, yet still manages to smell crisp and refreshing. I squint my eyes against the brilliant blue of the sky and shiver in delight as the heat of the sun is overcome by the chill of the wind. This day is distinctively autumn.

Yet for all the loveliness surrounding me, I almost forego my time on the porch. Work calls so loudly that I feel the need to stick my fingers in my ears. So much to do, so little time. But I know I need some time with God, so I take a seat on the swing.

I listen to the wind blowing through the trees and to the geese honking as they swim back and forth across the lake. As I sit, a neighbor boy rides through the yard on his bike. He comes to within a few feet of where I sit on the porch swing, but he's so intent on what he's doing that he doesn't even notice me.

He rides through the front yard, curling around the

pear tree and taking the curve around the weeping cherry tree with the determination of a race car driver. I open my mouth to let him know I'm here, but I shut it again and watch instead. Over and over he circles the pear tree, goes around the cherry tree, heads to the backyard, then comes back to circle the pear and cherry trees.

As I take this in, I sense how much like that boy I am. Although I want to deny that truth, many days I'm so intent on what I'm doing, I'm not even aware that God is waiting for me to join Him for our special time on the porch. So many days, He waits alone. That picture of my heavenly Father sitting by Himself sears itself into my brain, and my heart aches. Today was almost one of those days. This moment, this epiphany, was almost one I missed.

Prayer: Heavenly Father, send Your Holy Spirit to teach me to love You in such a way that our time together becomes like food and drink to me. Without those, as without You, I am unable to live. In Jesus' name. Amen.

Reflection: What has taken your focus off the Lord or interrupted your time with Him?

Yours, O LORD, is the greatness and the power and the glory and the majesty and the splendor, for everything in heaven and earth is Yours.
(1 Chronicles 29:11)

THE POWER OF GOD

The wind is growing stronger this afternoon, and I watch its gusts pull the leaves from the highest branches of the trees and drop them quickly to the ground. The fallen leaves mingle with the last few flower petals that have been stripped from their stems. Out in the yard, Emily raises her arms and turns her face toward the wind. "It's pushing me!" she shouts as she leans her tiny body into the breeze and tries to make headway against its steady current. "Come here, Mom!" she calls. "Hurry!"

I leave the porch to join my daughter in the yard. The wind whips my hair around, covering my face, until I turn to face it head on. "There's a storm coming," I tell my daughter. "See how those dark gray clouds are racing across the sky?"

As if in confirmation, a fat raindrop splashes on my head. It's followed by another, then another. I grab Emily's hand, and we race for the covering of the porch. We each choose a rocking chair and watch as the wind blows the raindrops across the lake in sheets. Soon I feel a mist of water against my face.

"I'm going in," Emily declares.

"Wait just a minute," I tell her. I'm not yet ready to give up the fierce beauty of this storm. I want to continue to witness the power displayed before me—for I know it is the awesome power of God.

Too often I forget that my God is—God. I forget that He holds all power, knows all things, is present in all places at all times. Sometimes I lose sight of His awesome majesty. I get so caught up in the daily routine of my life that I forget that the God who loved me enough to send His Son to earn salvation for me on the cross also holds the universe in His hands. I forget that He is the God who spoke the world into being and who can raise up valleys and flatten mountains. Days like today give me just a small taste of God's power and help me put into perspective His strength and might.

Days like today also make me humbly grateful that a God so big and so strong has made someone as weak and small as me one of His beloved children.

Prayer: Heavenly Father, I praise You for the mighty ways You move over the earth. I praise You for the gift of Your Son to be my Savior. I praise You for the gift of faith and the many ways You work in my life. In Jesus' name. Amen.

Reflection: How have you seen the awesome power of God displayed recently?

I am with you and will watch over you. (Genesis 28:15)

BACK TO SCHOOL

Steven joins me on the porch this afternoon with his homework clutched in his hand. "Mom, I don't get this," he says as he sits next to me on the swing. School has been in session for a couple weeks now, and I've noticed that my youngest son is having some difficulty adjusting to his new routine. I hope this time together will provide an answer to the question of what's been bothering him.

"Which problem is it?" I ask, glancing over the work sheet.

Steven points to a story problem and graph. As I read, Steven periodically interrupts to have me further explain the parts he doesn't understand. When we finish going over everything, he carefully writes down his answer. Then, instead of leaving, he snuggles in closer.

"How's school?" I ask, wrapping my arm around him.

"Not good," he answers glumly.

"What's not good about it?"

"There's so much work," Steven says. "I never have time to play."

"Oh," I reply, biting my tongue so I don't remind him that he just spent an hour with his friends in the backyard. "Anything else?"

Steven pauses before answering. "Well, there are a lot of new kids in my class, we eat lunch really late, and we do things different than we did last year. I don't like it."

With a dawn of understanding, I realize Steven's trouble at school has to do with his resistance to change. My son has a take-it-slow personality that doesn't mesh well with all the new experiences the beginning of the school year brings. Adjusting to a new teacher, a new classroom, and a new grade level has left him out of sorts.

I weigh my words carefully before I speak. I share Steven's love of the status quo and understand his feelings all too well. Unfortunately for the two of us, life is full of change. This very season is a perfect example with its up-and-down temperatures, the bright, new colors on the trees, and the changing of time.

"Steven, I want you to look at me," I say as I slide my arm from around his shoulders. Steven turns.

"You're going to encounter a lot of new situations at school this year and each year as you get older," I tell my son. "I'll support you the best I can, but I want you to remember that God is with you in each new experience you face. The Lord promises that He'll be there to comfort you if you feel scared (Psalm 86:17). He'll be there to guide you if you have a hard decision to make (Proverbs 3:5, 6). He'll be there to walk beside you if you simply need a friend (Proverbs 18:24). He will forgive you when you make mistakes (1 John 1:9)." I pause to let my words sink in. "The Lord never asks us to go through anything alone. He's always with us. Do you understand?"

Steven nods.

I take his hand and sandwich it between mine. "Let's ask God to help you adjust to all the new things that are happening at school this year, okay?"

Steven nods again, and the two of us bow our heads. "Feel better?" I ask when we finish.

Steven nods.

I pull my son against me for a hug. In our embrace I feel God's reassurance that in each new situation we face, He will be there. Amid the changes of life, God will be steadfast and true. He promised.

Prayer: Father, I'm thankful for Your help in parenting my children. I praise You for the way You love and protect them even more than I do. In Jesus' name. Amen.

Reflection: What new situations is the Lord helping you walk through right now?

I, the LORD your God, am a jealous God. (Exodus 20:5)

TIME TOGETHER

A cool breeze blows across the porch, ruffling the pages of my open Bible. I've enjoyed my quiet time with God—offering up praise and prayers and reading from His Word—but now it's time to get on with my day. As I lay my marker across the page and start to close my Bible, I hesitate for a moment. I push aside thoughts of housework and writing deadlines and open my Bible again. Like Mary, my choice is to spend more time sitting at Jesus' feet.

Over the last few weeks the Holy Spirit has given me a renewed hunger for God's Word. Instead of the usual chapter or two that typically fills me up, I find myself devouring page after page of the Bible. As I do, God's plan of salvation and His love for me unfold before my eyes. With each verse, the Holy Spirit grants me fresh insights. With each chapter, He gives me new perspectives.

What has amazed me even more than the words I've read is the work God is doing in my heart. As I spend additional time reading my Bible, it's become clear to me that the Lord is eager to spend time with me. The apostle James writes: "Come near to God and He will come near to you" (James 4:8).

That thought amazes me. I am overwhelmed at the idea

that my heavenly Father might enjoy my company and savor the moments we share together. Over and over Scripture declares that my heavenly Father is a "jealous God" (Exodus 20:5) who loves me with an abiding love and who desires to have my full attention.

Each day as I come to this place to be with the Lord, I am shown "how wide and long and high and deep is the love of Christ" (Ephesians 3:18). Before such a love, I stand humbled and amazed. Because of such a love, I stand worthy and redeemed.

Prayer: Heavenly Father, increase my hunger for Your Word and for Your work in my life. In Jesus' name. Amen.

Reflection: What holds you back from spending more time with the Lord?

Rejoice in the Lord always. Again I will say it: Rejoice!
(Philippians 4:4)

AUTUMN JOY

From the porch steps I watch Micah and Emily at work under the maple trees in the front yard. Armful by armful they heap fallen leaves into a pile that resembles a small mountain. The two of them have been working for quite a while, and I'm surprised to see they're still busy.

Then, at a signal from Micah, the two let out ear-splitting whoops and leap into the mound. Leaves fly in all directions. Some are caught by the breeze and lifted back to the treetops while others rain down to settle in my children's hair and on their clothes like the newest in fall fashion apparel. After all their work, the time for fun has finally arrived. The two of them make the most of it.

My children's joy is contagious, and I feel my spirits lift as I watch their antics.

Sometimes I get so caught up in my work—as a wife, mother, writer, church volunteer, and school helper—that I forget to stop for moments of fun. It's during these times that my faith walk turns into drudgery, and the Lord becomes a heavenly recorder, listing each infraction I commit. The last few weeks have been one of those times.

My focus lately has been on the "thou shalt nots" of

God's Word. While the Ten Commandments are a guide to my Christian conduct, God has given me wonderful promises in Scripture that tell me "I have done." These encourage me to celebrate with my thoughts, words, and actions the fact that the joy of the Lord is my strength (Nehemiah 8:10). As I search Scripture, I find precious gems that enable me to "rejoice in the Lord always" (Philippians 4:4) and to "shout for joy to the LORD ... worship the LORD with gladness; come before Him with joyful songs" (Psalm 100:1–2).

Watching my children has helped me see that God doesn't want me to plod through life. He has given me abundant blessings and wants me to celebrate the joy of all He has done for me. I rise from the porch steps with a new resolve to rejoice in all the Lord has given to me. I'll start by joining my children for some homemade joy right in my front yard.

Prayer: Heavenly Father, Your Word tells me, "Happy is that people, whose God is the LORD" (Psalm 144:15 KJV). Thank You for bringing me to faith in You so I may call You Lord of my life and rejoice in Your presence on a daily basis. In Jesus' name. Amen.

Reflection: What joyful experience has the Lord given you recently?

Do you not know that in a race all the runners run,
but only one gets the prize? Run in such a way as to get the prize.
(1 Corinthians 9:24)

THE RACE

From my seat on the porch, I see Steven and Matt, an older boy from the neighborhood, at the top of our driveway. From my son's stance, I know he's challenging Matt to a race.

In the past week, Steven has discovered the joy of running. Along with that, he's decided that he's quick as a fox and faster than lightning. When his boasting starts, a challenge is usually not far behind. "I'll race you!" he says with the confidence of a winner.

Surprisingly, it doesn't matter if the person being challenged is several years older and a foot taller than Steven— my son still thinks he'll win. This week I've seen him race his brother more times than I can count. He's lost every contest, but it still hasn't stopped him from putting forth the challenge. Yesterday he even threw down the gauntlet with me as I walked to the mailbox. There was Steven on his bike offering to race me back down the driveway. "You run, and I'll ride," he said, hoping to better his chances.

"Okay," I told him, even though I knew this race leaned heavily in his favor.

"On your mark, get set, GO!" he called.

I started out in front for a short distance. Once his bike got rolling, Steven pulled ahead. "I win!" he shouted as he reached the house before me. I smiled, happy to share in his victory.

Now as I watch my son take on his latest challenge, I admire his tenacity. He's not shy about giving this his all. When it comes to racing—as with most other things in life—Steven doesn't give up. He tries his hardest and runs with a determination to do his best. If he doesn't win this time, there's always the next time.

As Steven's latest race unfolds before my eyes, I can't help but wish some of his desire to run would rub off on me. Lately I seem to be trudging through my Christian walk. I attend church, participate at the Lord's table, read my Bible, and say my prayers, but I know I'm not "running in such a way as to get the prize" (1 Corinthians 9:24). For weeks now, I've felt like I'm just going through the motions. My mind wanders during my pastor's sermon, my prayers are halfhearted, and my quiet time is inconsistent. Even today my Bible sits unopened on my lap. I feel as though I have lost sight of the finish line in this race.

As Matt sprints ahead to win his race with Steven, I can see my son gesturing that he wants a rematch. There's no giving up, He doesn't walk away without trying again. He doesn't quit. There's a lesson here for me.

The apostle writes: "Let us run with perseverance the race marked out for us. Let us fix our eyes on Jesus, the Author and Perfecter of our faith, who for the joy set before Him endured the cross" (Hebrews 12:1–2). Steven has shown that kind of perseverance so many times over the past week. Although he's been handed defeat after defeat, he's always willing to try again.

I take a deep breath and open my Bible. Today I, too, am ready for the challenge. I want to continue the race. I am eager to compete, determined to do my best, confident of victory—because my eyes are fixed on Jesus.

Prayer: Heavenly Father, when the race seems long and hard, keep my feet from stumbling. When it feels like I've lost my way, be my guide. When the end is in sight, open Your arms to receive Your child. In Jesus' name. Amen.

Reflection: How is the Holy Spirit helping you to run the race in such a way as to get the prize?

"Come to Me, all you who are weary and burdened, and I will give you rest." (Matthew 11:28)

HELP WITH MY BURDENS

Besides the brilliant red, sunny yellow, and vibrant orange leaves on the trees surrounding the lake, there is another color to autumn lately—gray. For the past few days the sun has hidden behind nickel-colored clouds and a misty rain has fallen. "Can't You drive these clouds away, Lord?" I mutter as I sit on the swing.

I feel a new kinship to David when I read the words he spoke to God: "Be merciful to me, O LORD, for I am in distress" (Psalm 31:9). I shake my head a little as I realize the "distress" of my life is much different than David's, much smaller. David was running from King Saul and his attempts to end David's life. I only want to run from all those commitments that are adding stress to mine. The school year has just started and already I'm feeling overwhelmed by all the worthwhile things to which I've said yes—PTA committees, fund-raisers at two schools, classroom duties, field trips. I sigh, knowing the list doesn't even include my obligations at church and to my writing.

While I know God never gives us more than we can handle, I also know that God hasn't exactly given me these things. I've taken each task of my own free will by saying yes when I should have said no. Somehow I've convinced myself I'm the only person to do the job right. Now the weight of my commitments feels staggering and burdensome.

I'm tired and weary, and, unreasonably, I want a visible sign of God's presence. I want to know He's walking with me through this maze of commitments I've taken on. As I read further in the psalm for today, a verse catches my eye: "Let Your face shine on your servant" (Psalm 31:16a). *That's it!* I think. *Break through those rain clouds with some brilliant sunshine, Lord! Show me You're here!*

The wind picks up, and the clouds begin to move. *Here comes the sun!* I think. But the sun stays hidden. But I don't feel disappointed. Instead, I have peace and satisfaction because I know that spectacular displays from God don't strengthen my faith—only the Holy Spirit does through God's Word. The fact is that God sent His Son, Jesus, so I might be His child. Because I am His child, I trust that Jesus walks beside me day by day.

My heart rejoices as I read to the end of today's psalm: "Be strong and take heart, all you who hope in the LORD" (Psalm 31:24). Today and everyday my hope is in the Lord. I feel my burdens lift as God's strength fills my heart.

Prayer: Father, even when the sun doesn't peek out from behind the clouds, I know I am always in the sunshine of Your love. Thank You for carrying my burdens. Help me to say no when necessary. Send Your Holy Spirit to strengthen me for the tasks ahead. In Jesus' name. Amen.

Reflection: What burdens are you carrying that you can give to the Lord?

The gift of God is eternal life in Christ Jesus our Lord.
(Romans 6:23)

SPECIAL DELIVERY

As I sit on the porch this afternoon, Emily is pedaling slowly around the driveway on her bicycle. Every so often she climbs off the bike, picks up a leaf or a pretty rock, and brings it over to where I sit. "Special delivery!" she announces as she places her latest treasure in my hand so I can share in her discovery.

"How wonderful!" I say each time, giving her a moment to tell me about what she's found. "This *is* a special delivery!"

Before long, Emily hurries back to her playing. I smile as I remember years past when Micah and Steven were little, and both of them would play this same game with me. How quickly the time has flown by.

After several deliveries, Emily climbs the porch steps again and stands before me. "Yes?" I say, putting out my hand to take her latest offering. This time, though, Emily motions with her finger for me to lean toward her. As I do, she places her arms around my neck and kisses me softly on the cheek. "Special delivery!" she says gleefully, hardly able to contain her joy.

I scoop her up into my lap and return her kiss with one

of my own. "Special delivery to you too!" I say, holding my daughter close to my heart.

"I love you, Mom," Emily tells me, the sound muffled against my chest.

"I love you too, my girl," I reply, delighted to be the recipient of all this affection.

My daughter's words and actions warm my heart and speak to me of a childlike love that, at times, I know I don't deserve. Time after time I'm grateful that my children are able to look past my impatience and my anger. Despite my imperfections as a mother, they love me.

I'm even more grateful that my heavenly Father loves me. Because I am washed in the blood of Jesus, the Lord draws me close to His heart and whispers "I love you!" in my ear. This is the same "I love you!" that was shouted from the cross when God's own Son, Jesus, died for my sins. Jesus' sacrifice done out of love has bridged the gap between me and my heavenly Father. Of all the gifts I've ever received, that one is by far the most special delivery.

Prayer: Heavenly Father, thank You for sending Your only Son to die for me, a sinner. Amen.

Reflection: What is one way God has shown His love for you recently?

But because of His great love for us, God, who is rich in mercy,
"made us alive with Christ even when we were dead in transgressions
—it is by grace you have been saved. (Ephesians 2:4)

EMPTY-HANDED

The ducks greet me exuberantly as they see me walk onto the front porch. In a flash they're waddling across the hardening ground in hopes of an afternoon meal for which they don't have to work. I hate to disappoint them, but I hold up my hands. "Sorry, but I don't have anything this time," I say.

I take my place on the swing as the ducks mill around, quacking their objections at the bottom of the porch steps. It's as if they still hope I'll pull some food out of my pocket and throw it down to them. Most mornings when I come out to the porch, I do have some old bread, rolls, or popcorn for the ducks, but in the afternoons, I'm empty-handed.

Today I'm struck by how aptly that describes my Christian life. Day after day as I come before my heavenly Father, I relearn a very simple truth: "For it is by grace you have been saved through faith—and this not of yourselves, it is the gift of God—not by works, so that no one can boast" (Ephesians 2:8–9).

When I come before God, I come empty-handed.

There is nothing I can do to impress the Lord. There is no act of courage or kindness, no good deed, no selfless feat that brings me any closer to earning His favor. To God, my acts of righteousness "are like filthy rags" (Isaiah 64:6). In a world that loves to reward good deeds done by good people, God's gift of unmerited grace is beyond understanding. How incredible, as one of the Lord's own, to know that my worth isn't wrapped up in what I do or who I am— instead it's all wrapped up in the act of a Child who was born in a stable, died on a tree, and rose again to declare He saved the world.

As the apostle tells all of God's children: "Let us then approach the throne of grace with confidence, so that we may receive mercy and find grace to help us in our time of need" (Hebrews 4:16). God's throne is approachable. His gift of grace is free for all.

Prayer: Father, what an overwhelming gift Your grace is to me! Thank You for making me Your child through the waters of Baptism that I may enjoy the blessings of Jesus' saving work on the cross. In Jesus' name. Amen.

Reflection: How will you demonstrate your thankfulness to God for His free gift of grace?

But God demonstrates His own love for us in this:
While we were still sinners, Christ died for us. (Romans 5:8)

TRUE LOVE

Today is beautiful and sunny, just the opposite of the gray, wet day my niece had for her wedding this past weekend. Despite the weather, the bride looked radiant, and the groom stood tall and handsome as they declared their love for and commitment to each other. Their wedding has left me thinking about love.

In junior high I remember the thrill of running into my latest "crush" in the hall or spying him across the crowded cafeteria. At that time in my life, love was the giddy feeling I got when the young man of the moment looked my way.

In senior high I did more longing for love than anything else. Most of my friends were involved in dating relationships, but I wasn't. Although my mom assured me my day would come, I was sure that love had passed me by.

During college, love literally came knocking on my door. I had just returned from Christmas break when Tim passed by the open door of my dormitory room and saw me unpacking. He came back, knocked on the door, and introduced himself. A week later we went on our first date. A year and a half later we were married.

Since those early days I've learned quite a bit about

what love is—and what it isn't. Over the years that Tim and I have been married, I've learned that while love is about warm feelings and tender moments, it is also about commitment, work, and sacrifice. That wasn't the romantic notion I had when I walked down the aisle to the man of my dreams. But I wouldn't change one thing about the love Tim and I share today. After all these years the romance is still alive, and the love has grown deeper. I like it this way.

Eighteen years ago, Tim and I made a commitment to each other. On that sunny June day we vowed that our marriage was "for richer, for poorer, in sickness and in health, till death do us part." We took that vow seriously then, and we still take it seriously now because we know that our union has been joined by God. We asked the Lord's blessing on our marriage and vowed to carry out that which He blessed.

Now there are daily opportunities to "walk in love" (Ephesians 5:2 KJV)—to put each other first, to act kindly at the end of a hard day, to show love when we don't feel love, to forgive as we have been forgiven by God. What makes our choice to stay committed to each other easier is that we have the example set by Jesus. Christ displayed a love for us that was sacrificial and unconditional. It is a love that literally gave itself for others. That is the standard we hold up for ourselves—the goal we strive for. We both know we can never attain this perfect love, but with the Holy Spirit's help we can forgive each other and move forward in love with Christ at the center of our marriage.

On this beautiful, sunny day I remember a wedding, a

vow, a commitment, a sacrifice—and I think about love.

Prayer: Jesus, Your death on the cross shines forth to the world as the ultimate expression of love. Thank You that Your sacrifice gives us forgiveness of sins and that Your resurrection guarantees us eternal life. Amen.

Reflection: What person in your life needs a special reminder of God's love?

If any of you lacks wisdom, he should ask God, who gives generously to all without finding fault, and it will be given to him. (James 1:5)

FILLING GOD'S SHOES

I've been out in the yard most of the afternoon, planting some new bushes along the fence line. My garden boots are covered with mud, so I slip them off as I climb the porch steps for a short break.

Emily rounds the corner of the house and sees my boots sitting there. I already can tell what she's going to do, and she doesn't disappoint me. As soon as she reaches the boots, she slides her feet into them and looks at me with an impish grin. "I have your shoes on!" she sings as she takes a few awkward steps forward. "I'm the mom!"

"Be careful that you don't fall," I warn her. "Those are awfully big for you."

"I won't fall," she says, then promptly struggles to regain her balance.

My daughter is like me in so many ways. We both have straight brown hair and dark brown eyes. We both have wide, toothy smiles and friendly dispositions. This time, though, Emily's actions show me a part of myself I hope she doesn't take after—my tendency to try to fill other people's shoes.

I often jump into things with both feet. Usually that's

okay, but sometimes I find out too late that I've jumped in over my head. Instead of admitting that I need help, I'll proudly struggle forward on my own. It doesn't matter to me that my talents or abilities may not line up with the task I'm trying to accomplish, I just grit my teeth and move on, stumbling and falling the whole way as I try to fill up shoes that are just too big for me. I've learned the hard way that "pride goes before destruction, a haughty spirit before a fall" (Proverbs 16:18).

Even worse, though, have been those times when I've tried to fill up God's shoes. Times like when a friend has come to me for advice and I promptly respond with what I would do instead of turning with her to God for His answers as we search His Word and lay our needs before Him in prayer. It's times like that when I can picture myself standing before my heavenly Father foolishly wearing a pair of oversized shoes I will never be able to fill—because they belong to Him.

Whether it's my prideful nature or my tendency to move forward without first seeking God's direction that causes me to stumble and fall, I often end up with my feet slipping out from under me. Instead of getting up again, I can ask the Holy Spirit to help me slide off those oversized shoes I'm wearing, rise only to my knees, and ask the Lord for His forgiveness, His help, and His guidance.

Prayer: Father, please guide me in the ways I should go. Forgive me for Jesus' sake for the times I try to fill Your "shoes." In His name I pray. Amen.

Reflection: Whose shoes are you trying to fill?

We will tell the next generation the praiseworthy deeds of the LORD.
(Psalm 78:4)

FRONT PORCH STORIES

I remember as a child sitting with my father and asking him to tell me stories of when he was a boy. My request usually was granted with tales of daring adventures and near escapes from outlandish situations. Never mind that I didn't quite know if those stories were completely believable. One day my dad even taught me the official song he wrote for a pirate club he formed with his brother when they were boys. From then on we'd sing it together while we were driving in the car or out in the yard.

Listening to my father's stories would transport me to a world I didn't know—a world I could only see through his eyes. Yet by the time the stories were finished, it was a shared vision. I knew my father a little better and felt like part of his world.

These days it is my own children asking me for stories and wanting to share my childhood. "Tell us about when you were a little girl," Steven asks as he, Micah, Emily, and I huddle on the swing in the cool of the late afternoon. I let my mind wander to when I was young and watch as story after story unfolds. I choose from the vast library of memories and begin.

I tell them about the bakery truck that came down our street every Saturday morning with pastries for the adults and shelf after shelf of penny candy for the kids. As hard as I try, I can't begin to describe the wonderful smell that filled my nose and the sense of anticipation that filled my heart as I climbed the steps of the truck and stood in front of all that candy.

I tell them, too, about the time I gave in to a friend's challenge and jumped from the limb of a tree while holding a piece of rope that was tied to another branch. We both thought that by jumping from the tree I would sail higher than anyone had ever sailed before. Instead, the rope wrapped around my finger, and the force of the jump caused it to tighten and almost slice off my fingertip. I still remember running home to my mom with tears dripping down my cheeks and blood dripping down my hand.

Besides my own stories, I share the stories I heard from my father when I was a child. When I'm finished, there are cries of "Did that really happen?" I smile and let them wonder.

Our time of storytelling reminds me of the importance of learning from the generations that came before so we can teach the generations to come. So in between the stories from my past, I intertwine stories of our present. These are stories of courage, faith, and love taken from the pages of the greatest book of all—the Bible.

My children hear of the faith of Abraham, who trusted God even to the point of being willing to sacrifice his son, Isaac. They hear of the courage of Moses as he stood up to

Pharaoh and demanded that God's people be granted their freedom. They hear of the love of a Father who sacrificed His only Son for the sake of all people (John 3:16).

By telling stories of fun, and family, and faith, I hope to leave a legacy of love to my children. I want them to understand their past, enjoy their present, and anticipate their future. I want to enrich the lives of my children with all kinds of stories. I want them to know, too, that the most important stories they can ever learn are the stories passed down from their heavenly Father.

Prayer: Father, the story I never tire of hearing is the story of Your love for me. Tell me again, won't You? In Jesus' name. Amen.

Reflection: What are some special stories from the Bible and from past generations that you can share with your children?

Carry each other's burdens, and in this way you will fulfill the law of Christ.
(Galatians 6:2)

ISOLATION

From my swing, I see a lone Canada goose sitting under the trees in the front yard. When the bird landed here about a month ago, our family soon noticed that it stayed apart from the other ducks and geese. Micah and Steven went to investigate and quickly discovered why. Someone had shot an arrow at the goose, piercing its body and pinning its rear leg against its side. For days, neighbors joined us as we tried to capture the animal so the arrow could be removed. No matter what we tried, we were never fast enough. The goose would either fly into the lake or flap its wings to skirt across the grass to another part of the yard. Finally we gave up.

After a few days the bird disappeared—only to reappear a week later with the arrow gone, its body bloody and swollen, and its leg bent uselessly against its side. We all watched as the goose hobbled around on one leg, still keeping apart from the rest of the birds on the lake. While the others would fly off and return, the injured goose stayed put.

"I wonder if we're going to have a permanent visitor this winter," I mentioned to Tim one afternoon as the weather turned colder and the goose gave no sign of leaving.

"I don't think so," he replied. "It's just recovering."

Now each day as I come out to the porch swing, I notice the increasing chill to the air. I also notice the goose continuing to sit by itself. *Why didn't it let us help?* I question. *Why is it still isolating itself?*

I should know the answers to those questions from personal experience. So often when I'm feeling sick or hurt, I pull apart from my friends and family and refuse all offers of assistance, thinking I can take care of everything by myself.

"Are you sure there isn't something we can do?" others ask.

"No, thanks. I'll be fine," I tell them. "I can manage on my own."

What I fail to realize is that not only am I depriving myself of the caring, comfort, and help I so sorely need, but I also am depriving others of the opportunity to put their faith into action by "[carrying] each other's burdens" (Galatians 6:2).

When I withdraw, not only am I turning away from my family and friends, I'm also turning away from God. Why would the Father who loves me more than anyone else refuse to help me when the Bible clearly tells me He's "a refuge for the poor, a refuge for the needy in his distress, a shelter from the storm, and a shade from the heat" (Isaiah 25:4)?

God doesn't mean for me to carry my pain, my hurt, and my sorrow alone. He's given me a community of believers who are there to help me bear my burdens. Even more than that, He's given me Himself.

Prayer: Heavenly Father, sometimes it's hard to be on the receiving end of help—whether it's the help of friends and family or Your help. Thank You that there are those who care enough to offer time and energy when I need it. Thank You that You care enough to reach into my isolation and draw me near. In Jesus' name. Amen.

Reflection: How can God help you to be more receptive when others offer their help?

Find rest, O my soul, in God alone; my hope comes from Him. He alone is my rock and my salvation; He is my fortress, I will not be shaken.
(Psalm 62:5–6)

SEEKING GOD'S WILL

The weather has turned much colder over the last few nights. Each morning the ground is white with frost, and each afternoon the air smells of snow and winter. This afternoon is no exception, and there is even a thin layer of ice around the edges of the pond.

I smile at the white ducks. Their winter feathers have come in, and the new plumpness to their bodies makes them look like they're wearing fluffy new coats as protection from the bitter cold to come. Around the lake, the Canada geese are restless, and there is a lot of activity among the flock. While some swim the perimeter, others walk along the edges. A few of them call back and forth to one another—their usual signal before taking flight.

Over the last few days I've seen the V-formation of other flocks of geese flying over our house as they make their way to warmer climates. I know our geese will soon follow. It's time to say good-bye for the season. Suddenly the noise around the lake increases as more geese add their calls to the rest. Then, with a beating of wings, the birds are airborne, the brownish-gray of their bodies reflected in the dreary gray of the sky. They circle the lake once, then turn southward. I know it will be many months before I see them again.

A sense of sadness comes over me. I wasn't ready to give up the colorful days of autumn, but today I know I have no choice. The trees are bare, the sun has lost its warmth, and now the geese are gone. Winter is not far off.

Part of me wishes I could spread my wings and follow the geese to a place where the sun shines brightly, and the breeze blows soft and sweet. Today there is a restless feeling in my spirit. Do You have something different for me, God? I wonder.

The wind blows, and a few dry, brown leaves skirt across the grass in front of me. I sit quietly, realizing this may be a prayer God doesn't answer right away. As I wait, I will hold onto Jesus' promise: "Your Father knows what you need before you ask Him" (Matthew 6:8). After all, God knew my greatest need and sent Jesus to redeem me and bring me into His family forever. So I will wait in hope, knowing the Lord has heard my prayer and He is working.

Prayer: Father, I want to do Your will and walk in Your way. Direct my life in Your perfect path. In Jesus' name. Amen.

Reflection: How will you ask God to help you continue to seek His will?

*So then, just as you received Christ Jesus as Lord, continue to live in Him,
rooted and built up in Him, strengthened in the faith as you were taught,
and overflowing with thankfulness. (Colossians 2:6–7)*

GIVING THANKS

The coolness of the air outside is a wonderful respite
after the hours I've spent in the heat of the kitchen. Today
is Thanksgiving Day, and the house is filled with the smell
of turkey cooking in the oven and pumpkin pies cooling on
the counter. This year it's my turn to host my family's fall
get-together, and there's plenty to do.

Once I count all those who will be here later this afternoon—my mom, my sisters and brothers, and their families—the number hits 30 and climbs steadily higher. This is
a day that will stretch our home to its seams with the
enthusiasm of a big family. There will be noise, confusion,
joy, laughter, helping, sharing, merriment—and love. More
than anything, there will be love.

Now, though, it's time to step back from the preparations of the day and take a few minutes to do some preparations in my heart. The cool breeze calms my spirit, and
the rhythm of the porch swing becomes a steady accompa-
niment as I count my blessings. I don't need a pencil and a
sheet of paper for this list because it is etched in my mind
and written on my heart.

This day I am grateful for the simple things: the faithful

love of my husband, Tim; the confident maturity I see in Micah; the enthusiasm for life I see in Steven; and the caring and compassion I see in Emily. I am thankful, too, for my family and friends, for my health, for my church, for Tim's job, for good teachers who care about my children, for my home ...

My list stretches on and on as I try to remember to thank God for each blessing, big and little, that He has graced my life with and for each moment of serendipity that this year has held. For each one, I know, is a "good and perfect gift" (James 1:17) given to me by my heavenly Father.

More than anything else today, I am thankful to God for His Son and for the forgiveness and life He gives to me. Because the Holy Spirit is at work in my life, I'm sharing Jesus' love with those around me as I focus on the needs of others instead of being absorbed with my own needs. I'm learning to live my life with "love, joy, peace, patience, kindness, goodness, faithfulness, gentleness, and self-control" (Galatians 5:22, 23). I'm learning to be thankful for each day as He helps me live in a way that pleases the Lord.

The psalmist says: "Give thanks to the LORD for He is good; His love endures forever" (Psalm 106:1). God is good, and His enduring love is the gift I am most thankful for on this Thanksgiving Day.

Prayer: Heavenly Father, on this day and every day, I thank You for Your merciful love and Your gracious care in providing for all my needs. In Jesus' name. Amen.

Reflection: What is at the top of your list of things you will thank God for today?

"Peace I leave with you; My peace I give to you."
(John 4:27)

A MOMENT OF PEACE

Tonight I flee to the front porch to find a small piece of sanity in my otherwise chaotic world. Between children fighting and music blaring, I've had all I can handle for the moment. It's as though Tim doesn't exist because suddenly everyone needs Mom. If it isn't Emily tugging at my sleeve to ask me to play or to get her a drink or to find the toy she's lost, it's the boys asking me for help with homework or to settle a dispute between the two of them. Some days knowing that my children still need me is flattering. Today, it's been exhausting.

I grab my Bible and head for the porch swing. I need a few minutes to settle down and calm my spirit. I want to bring my day before the Lord and ask for His strength to make it through until the end. I want to "be still, and know that [He is] God" (Psalm 46:10).

A few moments of peace and quiet are all I ask—yet I find them elusive. The inside of my head is noisy even though the porch is quiet. I thought I'd rush out here and pour out the events of my day to gain some perspective on things from the Lord, but I don't. Instead I find myself sitting very still, waiting—and hoping—for the quiet outside to still the noise inside my mind.

I close my eyes as a cool breeze blows across the porch. Its gentle touch against my cheek is like a soft caress. I sigh and slowly I feel the tension leave my body and the quietness around me permeate my spirit. Each time I come to this place, I have a deeper understanding of what it means that God is "my refuge and strength" (Psalm 46:1). Here in this place I feel safe, sheltered, and protected. Here I am reminded again and again that His grace is sufficient to meet all my needs—even a need as small as this one.

As I sit, my mind stills and my heart opens. There are times when I don't need help or answers from God—I only need His peace and His presence.

Prayer: Heavenly Father, amidst the noise of my life, thank You for reminding me that in You is quietness and strength. In Jesus' name. Amen.

Reflection: When was the last time you were quiet before the Lord?

Let everything that has breath praise the Lord.
(Psalm 150:6)

AUTUMN'S BLESSINGS

In the cold of the late autumn evening, I sit in the dark with my coat wrapped tightly around me. I haven't quite adjusted to the time change yet—that seasonal ritual when the hands on the clock are turned back an hour and darkness arrives shortly after 5 P.M.

The days pass quickly now, leaving less and less time for a quiet moment alone with the Lord. Once the boys arrive home from school, the rest of the day passes in a blur of doing for others. Tonight, though, I sneak out to the porch when no one is looking. Autumn is almost over, and I want to spend a few moments thinking back over the blessings this season has brought with it. Mostly I remember simple things:

- Frosty mornings when the grass sparkles like diamonds.

- The blazing beauty of autumn trees as they don their party best for one last celebration before the year is over.

- Seeing my breath for the first time in the cold morning air.

- The shouts of my children as they jump in the enormous pile of leaves they've spent the afternoon raking.

- Gold, orange, red, and purple leaves dancing in the wind.

- The crisp breeze that reduces the heat of the golden fall sunshine.

- The chattering of squirrels as they stop to play in the midst of gathering nuts for the winter.

- Apple trees lowering their branches to offer the abundant fruit they bear.

- The smell of a freshly baked pumpkin pie.

- Dry leaves that sound like crumpling newspaper as you walk through them.

- The smell and crackle of the campfire as the children search for sticks to roast marshmallows.

- The thankful feeling of family gathered around the table to count blessings.

- The pumpkin-colored moon at night.

For me, autumn is a time of abundance—the abundance of harvest, the abundance of nature's beauty, and the abundance of God's blessings. This evening I want to remember and savor every golden moment of the season because I know that soon the store of perfect days will be used up. Until then, I turn my face to the heavens to thank and praise my Father above for His autumn blessings.

Prayer: Heavenly Father, I praise You for this season of abundance. I join with all of Your creation in praising You, the Creator of all. In Jesus' name. Amen.

Reflection: How have you experienced God's abundant blessings in simple ways this season?

CHRISTMAS

The Season of My Savior

*For God so loved the world that He gave His one and only
Son, that whoever believes in Him shall not
perish but have eternal life.
(John 3:16)*

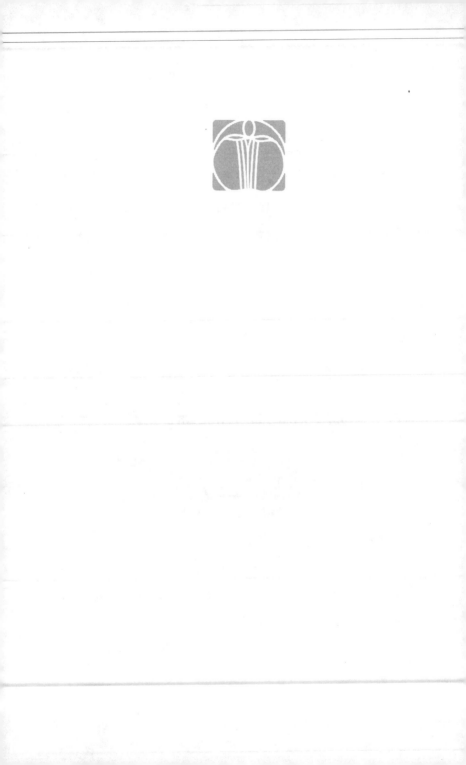

Prepare the way for the Lord. (Luke 3:4)

PREPARING FOR THE SAVIOR

I lean back into the porch swing, exhausted. I have been up since early this morning and have spent most of the day decorating our home for the Christmas season. First, the tree went up with its strings of white lights and collection of well-loved ornaments. Then I arranged our nativity, set out the rest of the seasonal decorations, and hung our Christmas pictures. After that I moved outside. While Tim was on the roof putting up our lights, I looped pine roping from porch post to porch post and tied each loop with a large maroon ribbon.

Our home is now decked out in its Christmas best and ready for the holiday season. But am I?

After this flurry of energy and activity, I know with certainty that I have neglected one thing—to truly prepare myself for Christmas. While I've put out the trappings of the season, I haven't "prepared the way for the Lord" (Luke 3:4). That happens in my heart.

I return to the house for my Bible and carry it back to the porch with me. Once I'm settled on the swing again, I turn to the story of Christ's birth in the Gospel according to Luke and read: "In those days Caesar Augustus issued a decree that a census should be taken of the entire Roman world" (Luke 2:1).

I feel my spirit calm and my tiredness lift as I read the words that soothe me with their familiarity. No matter how many times I hear the Christmas story, it never fails to move me. I catch my breath at the angel's proclamation of "good news of great joy that will be for all the people" (Luke 2:10), and I join with the heavenly host in praising God and saying, "Glory to God in the highest" (Luke 2:14).

This, indeed, is an event worth celebrating.

More than anything else this Christmas season, I want to be like the shepherds who journeyed to Bethlehem in search of their Savior. For me, though, the journey won't be far. With Christ in my heart, I know my Savior is always with me.

Prayer: Father, help me to be truly prepared to celebrate the birth of Your Son, Jesus. Bless my hands to do Your work, bless my thoughts to know Your will, bless my heart to love as You love me. In my Savior's name. Amen.

Reflection: How will you ask the Holy Spirit to help you to better prepare your heart for Jesus this Christmas season?

Set up road signs; put up guideposts. (Jeremiah 31:21)

CHRISTMAS TRADITIONS

Today the lake looks as though it has been sprinkled with the same powdered sugar that dusts the countertops and kitchen floor inside the house. Micah, Steven, Emily, and I have spent the morning baking Christmas cookies—sugar cookies in all shapes and sizes, snicker doodles, peanut butter cookies with a chocolate candy in the middle, chocolate chip cookies, and rosettes covered with powdered sugar.

After dusting ourselves off, we take a break from the mess and heat of the kitchen. While the children play in their rooms, I go out on the porch for a few quiet moments alone.

I love the traditions of Christmas. Baking cookies with my children is one of my favorites. Sometime in December I set aside a day when we can spend a few leisurely hours using our many cookie cutters to create festive holiday shapes. Micah puts the trays into the oven, and soon the entire house is filled with the sweet, sugary smell of baking cookies. After they're finished, we color icing and decorate our homemade creations. The best part, though, is sampling our efforts. I pour four cold glasses of milk, and we all treat ourselves to a few cookies from the delicious varieties we've made.

For my family, Christmas is full of such wonderful treats. They are our holiday traditions—those things, big and small, we do year after year that make our season special. For us, it wouldn't be Christmas without them.

Besides baking cookies, another tradition is counting down the days until Christmas with an Advent calendar that's posted on the front of the refrigerator. Each morning the children take turns opening a door on the calendar to reveal a symbol of the season. The more flaps that are open, the closer Christmas is.

At dinnertime the boys take turns carefully lighting the four candles—three purple and one pink—on our Advent wreath. As the wax pillars grow shorter, we make our way through the four weeks before our Savior's birth. Then on Christmas day we light the Christ candle, the white one in the center of the wreath.

These traditions are our "road signs" and "guideposts" (Jeremiah 31:21). They are the markers along our journey that let us know we are, indeed, traveling toward the light of Christmas and the celebration of a Child born in a stable who came to save the world from sin through His death on the cross.

Out here on the porch, I know our journey toward Christmas is just beginning. I look forward with joyful anticipation to the days ahead and pray that the traditions we celebrate will keep our eyes and hearts focused on Jesus.

Prayer: Jesus, flood my Christmas with Your presence so I may fully understand that the best part of this season is You. In Your precious name. Amen.

Reflection: What are some special Christmas traditions your family has and what do they mean to you?

And there were shepherds living out in the fields nearby,
keeping watch over their flocks at night.
An angel of the Lord appeared to them.
(Luke 2:8–9)

INTERRUPTIONS

"Mom, come see!" Emily calls from the top of the basement stairs.

I can tell by the tone of my daughter's voice that her request isn't urgent, so I ignore the interruption and continue wrapping presents behind a closed door.

"Not now, honey. I'm busy," I call.

I hear Emily's footsteps coming down the stairs, followed by a knock. "Come see!" she insists, her voice muffled as it floats through the door.

I look at the pile of presents around me and am tempted to refuse again. But the tug in my heart urges me to go. I open the door a crack and see the determined look on my daughter's face—now I know there's no use arguing. I slip out the door and give Emily my hand. "Let's go," I tell her.

Emily leads me upstairs to the front of the house. There she throws open the door to a world turning white. We step onto the porch to watch the snow fall. The flakes are so big it looks as though someone has opened a feather pillow and is shaking its fluffy, white contents down from the sky.

"God sent snow for Christmas!" Emily announces with delight. "Just like I asked."

"Thanks for showing me," I say. I stoop to give my daughter a hug. She wraps her arms around my neck, and I lift her up. The two of us stand together, sharing the joy of a child's wish fulfilled.

Too soon, Emily shivers with cold. "I want to go inside," she says.

"You go ahead," I tell her. "I'll be there in a minute."

As Emily disappears inside, I turn back to the scene before me. *This really was a lovely interruption, wasn't it, Lord?* I think. I haven't been too open to interruptions in my schedule lately. With the hustle and hurry of the Christmas season, I've been more apt to brush off my children's requests for a few minutes of my time. "I have too much to do" is my familiar refrain. "Not now, maybe later" is the chorus.

What if the shepherds had ignored the interruption of God's angel during their nightly task of tending sheep? What if they hadn't heeded the announcement and rushed to see the Baby? Think what they would have missed! They would not have traveled to Bethlehem to find "a baby wrapped in swaddling clothes and lying in a manger" (Luke 2:12). They may never have met their Savior face to face.

As I continue to watch the snow falling to the ground, I whisper a prayer that I will be more open to those moments when God chooses to interrupt the ordinary course of my day. I pray there will be more moments like this, moments when the Lord helps me see the joy and beauty of the season through the eyes of a child.

Prayer: Father, in the busyness of this holiday season, help me to be patient with life's interruptions—because so often they lead to special times spent with those I love. Help me also to be open to Your divine interruptions, when the nudge of Your Spirit bids me to take a break for the most important thing of all—time with You. In Jesus' name. Amen.

Reflection: In what ways has God "interrupted" your life recently?

Every good and perfect gift is from above. (James 1:17)

MAKING A LIST

I've brought my supplies to the porch with me this afternoon—pens, a yellow legal pad, and a handful of store and mail-order catalogs—to help with the task ahead of me. Today I'm making yet another Christmas list. Although presents are tucked away in secret places throughout the house, there are still some elusive gifts to be purchased for those hard-to-shop-for family members. I'm hoping the fresh air and sunshine will give me a new perspective for this task.

As I flip through the catalogs, I jot down a gift idea here, a store name there. My list doesn't grow very quickly, though, and I sigh in frustration. *Lord, as much as I love Christmas, this isn't my favorite part of the season,* I think.

After a few more minutes of turning pages, I flip to a fresh sheet of paper and begin a new list. I call it "Gifts I'd Really Like to Give This Christmas." At the top of the list I write Tim's name and the word *TIME* in bold, capital letters next to it.

My husband amazes me with all he can accomplish in a day, but I know his productivity has a cost. I can't remember the last time he had a few hours to get away and do something he enjoys—like shooting pictures or fly fishing or bike riding. If I could give Tim one gift this Christmas, it would be time for himself.

In that same spirit, I write a few more names on the paper and list the gifts I'd give each person if I could. For my children, I would give *contentment* to see them through the days after the holidays when friends begin the inevitable comparisons to what was found under their Christmas trees. For my mom, widowed now for a number of years, I wish for *peace* from the restlessness that has become part of her spirit since my father's death. For my sister, Lynn, a single mom, I put *strength enough for each day.* And the list continues.

When I finish writing, I pause for a moment before turning to a fresh page and starting yet another list. This new list is titled "Gifts God Is Giving/Has Given Me This Christmas." I close my eyes and relive moments and memories from the past few weeks. I remember the joy of sharing special times with special people. I remember the peace of kissing my children good night at the end of the day, knowing they were safe in God's care. I remember the love.

More than anything else, what has pervaded my Christmas season is the knowledge of God's great love for me. "For God so loved the world that He gave His one and only Son, that whoever believes in Him shall not perish but have eternal life" (John 3:16). Love moved God to give His Son to be laid in a manger and to die on a cross. Love caused Christ to take my sin to the cross as He sacrificed His life for mine. But this sacrifice of love didn't end at the grave; it continued on to a tomb made empty so all people would know that Jesus, the Christ, had risen victorious over death. Above all else, God's love means eternal life in Christ to me.

Prayer: Father, the gifts You continually give overwhelm me, yet none compares with the gift of Your Son. Thank You for sending Jesus to be my Savior. In His name I pray. Amen.

Reflection: How will you share God's gift of His Son with others this Christmas?

As for me, I watch in hope for the LORD, I wait for God my Savior.
(Micah 7:7)

EXPECTATIONS

Christmas is only a week away, yet I feel a sense of disappointment instead of a sense of joy.

All this month I've filled our weekends with visits from family and friends. Each one has helped us celebrate this season with love and laughter. I've spent hours making special foods—Swedish Timble cookies, eggnog, and pecan pie—that I only make at Christmas. I've had the house, tree, and porch decorated since the weekend after Thanksgiving. I've even arranged a few brightly colored packages under the tree.

But something is missing. I feel as though I have expectations that haven't been met this Christmas. What frustrates me is that I'm not sure what to do about it.

After wandering aimlessly around the house for a while—as if in search of some lost part of Christmas—I grab my coat and my Bible and head outside. I sit down on the porch steps and hug my Bible to my chest. "What am I missing, Lord?" I question. "Why does it feel as though there is a void in my celebration?"

I open my Bible, but instead of turning to the familiar Christmas story, I turn to the Book of Micah where Jesus' birth in the city of Bethlehem is foretold. As I read, a verse catches my eye and brings into focus the problem I am having this Christmas: "But as for me, I watch in hope for the LORD" (Micah 7:7).

I have been so caught up in the physical celebration of Christmas—with the gatherings and the food and the decorations—that I have forgotten about watching in hope for the one whose birth brings real meaning to my celebration. I've been focusing on the wrong thing. I've been wrapped up in celebrating the season instead of celebrating the Savior.

There on the porch, with my Bible open on my lap, I ask God to help me change the direction of my celebration and to turn my eyes in hopeful watchfulness for Him. God's promise from Lamentations settles quietly in my heart: "The LORD is good to those whose hope is in Him, to the one who seeks Him; it is good to wait quietly for the salvation of the LORD" (Lamentations 3:25–26).

At this moment, my Christmas season truly has begun as I celebrate the birth of Jesus, the one who is "the salvation of the LORD."

Prayer: Heavenly Father, help me to look past all those things that get in the way of focusing on Your gift of Jesus during this Christmas season. Help me to see clearly that Your Son is the reason I celebrate. In His name I pray. Amen.

Reflection: What things take your focus off of Jesus at Christmastime?

*All this took place to fulfill what the Lord had said through the prophet:
"The virgin will be with child and will give birth to a Son,
and they will call Him Immanuel"—which means, "God with us."
(Matthew 1:22–23)*

ANTICIPATION

The number of days until Christmas is growing shorter. So is the time between my children's impatient questions. How long will it be before the special day arrives?

"Is it Christmas yet?" Emily asks several times within the same hour. Her countdown has begun in earnest.

"No," I tell her, "there are still a few days left to wait." Earlier I tried to explain that Christmas is more like a season than a day, but Emily is too young to understand or to care. If it isn't the day when she gets to open her presents, it isn't the right day.

The boys are not quite so impatient, but I can feel their anticipation building too. I've noticed over the last few days they've done less fighting and more cooperating. There is a peaceful truce around the house.

I slide on my coat and head out to the front porch, craving a few minutes away from more questions. Yet even I feel a heightened sense of anticipation as the day of the Savior's birth draws near.

There are many things I'm looking forward to over the

next few days: the time I'll spend with family; the joy I'll see on the faces of those I love as presents are unwrapped and wishes are fulfilled; the meal we'll share as we gather around a table lit by the soft light of candles. But what I'm looking forward to the most is celebrating the greatest gift I've ever received—the gift of Immanuel, God with us.

As I sit on the swing, I'm surrounded by cold but warmed by God's love. It's a love that penetrates to my very soul as I am struck anew by the magnitude of God's gift: "For God so loved the world that He gave His one and only Son" (John 3:16). No longer was God separated from us by His perfection and our sin. Now God the Father had sent His Son to live here on earth, a human child, dwelling among us—a child who would grow up to take my sins to the cross and leave them there as He conquered sin, death, and Satan for me.

Sitting quietly, I hear the echo of my daughter's question, "Is it Christmas yet?" Although the day of celebration is still a few days away, I know Christmas is already here because today, as everyday, Jesus, Immanuel, is with me always.

Prayer: Oh come, Oh come, Emmanuel, and fill our hearts and our lives with Your Spirit, love, and forgiveness this Christmas day and every day. Amen.

Reflection: What part of your Christmas celebration do you look forward to the most? How is Jesus a part of this celebration?

"I am the Light of the world.
(John 8:12)

CHRISTMAS LIGHTS

This evening our family has enjoyed another of its annual Christmas traditions. Just as it begins to get dark, we pile into the van and head out to look at Christmas lights and displays.

For Micah, Steven, and Emily, the more lights the house has, the better they like it. We see two-story homes covered with string after string of large, colored lights; townhouses whose lawns are decorated with plastic snowmen and Santas; and a ranch house with a spotlighted nativity out front. There is even one family who has a Christmas greeting spelled out in small, white lights that cover the entire backyard.

"Can we do that next year?" someone asks. I shake my head.

As we drive on, we see houses covered only in white lights, others in only red, and one or two with only blue lights. The majority of houses, though, sport a rainbow of colors. Not only do these lights twinkle, they also blink off and on, chase one another, and cascade. After a couple hours spent driving all over town, I'm ready to rest my eyes.

Once the children have brushed their teeth and headed off to bed, I go out to the porch and sit on the steps. I turn my eyes to the dark night sky and notice there are not many stars out. What few there are can't begin to compare to the spectacular light displays we saw earlier.

But what am I seeking? The lights of the world or the Light of the world? While tonight's ride around town was fun, I know that the light of my Christmas season is Jesus Himself. He is the one who tells me: "I am the light of the world. Whoever follows Me will never walk in darkness, but will have the light of life" (John 8:12). As a follower of Christ, I also know I am called to let His light shine through me for others to see (Matthew 5:15–16).

This holiday season there will be many opportunities for my family and me to share God's love through our church, in our neighborhood, and with our friends. We will ask the Holy Spirit to help us take advantage of each opportunity and of this wonderful time of year to let our lights shine.

Prayer: Heavenly Father, fill me to overflowing with Your light and Your love so my life may be a shining reflection of You at Christmas and throughout the year. In Jesus' name. Amen.

Reflection: What are some practical ways you can shine the light of God's love on others?

"Give good gifts to your children." (Matthew 7:11)

THE GIFT

The house is dark around me except for the small, white lights that adorn the Christmas tree. Tim and I have just finished tucking the last of the presents under the tree's branches, but before we head upstairs to bed, the two of us slip outside to the porch to turn off the Christmas lights. With a pull of the plug, our house joins the rest of the darkened neighborhood. All around us, people have settled down for this long winter's night.

"Ready to go in?" Tim asks.

"I'll be right along," I say, wrapping my arms around myself for warmth. "I just need a minute."

Tim nods and goes inside.

I inhale the frosty air, then watch as my breath forms a cloud before me. I'm thankful for these few minutes alone to prepare my heart for tomorrow's celebration. And what a celebration it will be!

I know the stack of presents under the tree this year is bigger than usual, and I can just imagine the looks on my children's faces when they come down the stairs and see what awaits them. There will be shouts of joy and squeals of delight as the wrapping paper is torn away and long-awaited toys are found.

Yet the gift I want most to give my children this Christmas isn't one they'll find under the tree. This gift is one I've wrapped with love and tucked within my heart. It's a promise to myself, and to them, to give more of the "good gifts" (Matthew 7:11) that God intends for me to share—gifts like more of my time, more of my attention, and more of my patience, more of my forgiveness, more of our heritage as a family of faith.

I know from past experience what it means to my children when I put down what I'm doing and take a few minutes to enter their world. Reading a book together, playing a game, or listening to their favorite song carries the weight of a hundred "I love yous." I also know what it means to give them my full attention and really listen to what they have to say. I've seen their appreciation when I make the effort to maintain eye contact as they speak to me and to ask questions that let them know I've heard what they've said. I know the importance of modeling love, placing God first, and extending forgiveness as I teach them about the faith we hold dear.

Offering these gifts to my children will take some effort on my part. It will mean putting aside my priorities at times. It will mean obeying God's command to "love one another" (1 John 4:7) in a manner that my children can understand. It will mean taking the love and forgiveness God has shown me and extending it to my children in all our interactions.

It is this love that overwhelms me during this Christmas season as I think about God's great gift. I am amazed that "this is how God showed His love among us: He sent His one and only Son into the world that we might live through Him" (1 John 4:9). God knows all about giving good gifts to His children. Here on the porch I pledge to follow His example—not only at Christmas, but all through the year.

Prayer: Heavenly Father, You set an example of love and generosity for all of us in the gift You sent on that first Christmas day—the gift of Your Son, Jesus. Help us to give from our hearts as we extend to others the love You have shown to us. In Jesus' name. Amen.

Reflection: What good gifts would you like to give those you love this year?

For to us a Child is born, to us a Son is given, and the government will be on His shoulders. And He will be called Wonderful Counselor, Mighty God, Everlasting Father, Prince of Peace. (Isaiah 9:6)

SEASON OF MY SAVIOR

The family room floor is littered with the remains of Christmas. Pieces of torn wrapping paper and crumpled bows still decorate the carpet from our joyous evening celebration with Tim's family. I turn my back on the mess and walk out the front door, closing it firmly behind me. While Tim is upstairs putting the children in bed, I'll steal a few minutes on the porch.

I am greeted by a rush of cold air and the reassuring creak of the porch swing as I settle my weight on the seat. Today has been fun—but exhausting. It's been a day with presents to open, food to eat, stories to spin, memories to share, and good wishes to exchange. After a day so abundantly full, it feels good to sit back and relax.

As I sit, a new understanding fills me. With all the happiness that has been packed into this day, I realize why the celebration of Christmas begins right after Thanksgiving and extends into the new year. It's because the kind of joy this celebration holds is just too large to confine to 24 hours.

First, there are the four Sundays of Advent to heighten our anticipation and joy, strengthen our faith in God's promises, and focus our hearts and minds on the importance of Jesus' coming (both His first coming and His second). Then there are the 12 days of Christmas, that time from Christmas Day through Epiphany, when we reflect on the many gifts and blessings Jesus' birth has brought to this world.

Even more than the celebration, Christmas has grown from a day into a season because the magnitude of God's gift is too big to wrap up in only one day. The prophet Isaiah gave us a foreshadowing of the importance of Jesus' birth when he foretold that the baby to be born would be called "Wonderful Counselor, Mighty God, Everlasting Father, Prince of Peace" (Isaiah 9:6).

God wrapped Jesus in the frailty of a baby's skin and gave Him as a gift to the world so one day we might know the joy of life with our Father in heaven. And Mary "wrapped Him in swaddling clothes, and laid Him in a manger" (Luke 2:7 KJV). A humble beginning for heavenly royalty, but a humble life Jesus willingly took on for our salvation. He came that we might have eternal life in Him (John 3:16).

God's gift of His Son is truly too large to confine to only one day of joy and festivity. As I sit in the cold, I know this gift is one that takes a season to celebrate—the season of my Savior.

Prayer: Jesus, as we celebrate Your birth, help us to extend the love and joy of this time beyond the Christmas season so it encompasses our entire year. Amen.

Reflection: How will you celebrate your Savior at Christmas?

"My command is this: Love each other as I have loved you."
(John 15:12)

YEAR'S END

Today I have taken down the last of the pine roping and tucked away the maroon bows that have decorated the porch throughout the Christmas season. The rails look strangely bare without their holiday decorations, just as they do when I first take down the flower boxes that adorn them throughout the summer. I know this new look will take a few days to get used to, but I also know it's time to move forward into the new year.

A strong winter wind blows across the porch, rocking the swing in a silent invitation to sit down for a few moments. I gladly accept the offer.

Out in the yard I see the ducks swimming around on the half-frozen lake. As they go by, they *quack* their end-of-year greetings. At least for now they have the lake and yard to themselves—the mallards and Canada geese will likely not return until spring. The grass is brown and matted, and the branches of the maple trees that surround the lake are bare. Yet it looks like those same branches are being lifted to the sky in silent praise. This is, indeed, a day for giving God praise and glory for the year that has passed.

This year has held its share of happiness and heartache,

yet through each season God has shown me His love in abundant ways. Through winter, spring, summer, and fall, the Lord has strengthened my faith and affirmed His love as He has answered my prayers and moved in my life in His way and in His time. This year God has shown me over and over the abundant blessings He has laid out for me.

I know there is no way to repay the Lord for the year He has given me. There is nothing I can give Him that He doesn't already own because "the earth is the Lord's and everything in it" (1 Corinthians 10:26). Yet in the spirit of this giving season, I want to show God, in even a small way, my gratitude for all He has done in my life this year. I want the spirit of this Christmas season to extend throughout the year so lives are touched and changed. But how?

I smile as the answer comes to mind. "Love each other as I have loved you" (John 15:12). Today and everyday that I live, I will seek to love the Lord my God with all my heart and all my soul and all my strength (Deuteronomy 6:5). I will seek to share His love with others so they may know Him too, and by His Spirit, I will live my life in a way that reflects the Light of Christ to a world in need of His merciful love.

Prayer: Heavenly Father, though Christmas—and this year—are over, I rejoice that Your loving and forgiving presence in my life continues on into the new year. Send Your Holy Spirit to be my guide in the days ahead so I may walk in Your ways. In Jesus' name. Amen.

Reflection: As this year ends, how will you express your gratitude to God for all He has given you?